WILMA MANKILLER

NORTH AMERICAN INDIANS OF ACHIEVEMENT

WILMA MANKILLER
Principal Chief of the Cherokees

Melissa Schwarz

Senior Consulting Editor
W. David Baird
Howard A. White Professor of History
Pepperdine University

CHELSEA HOUSE PUBLISHERS

New York   Philadelphia

FRONTISPIECE   Principal Chief Wilma Mankiller prepares for a day's work in her office at the Cherokee Nation headquarters in Tahlequah, Oklahoma.

ON THE COVER   Wilma Mankiller, a leader whose energy and ideas have transformed Cherokee communities throughout eastern Oklahoma, was elected principal chief of the Cherokee Nation in 1987.

Chelsea House Publishers
EDITORIAL DIRECTOR   Richard Rennert
EXECUTIVE MANAGING EDITOR   Karyn Gullen Browne
COPY CHIEF   Robin James
PICTURE EDITOR   Adrian G. Allen
ART DIRECTOR   Robert Mitchell
MANUFACTURING DIRECTOR   Gerald Levine

North American Indians of Achievement
SENIOR EDITOR   Marian W. Taylor

Staff for WILMA MANKILLER
ASSISTANT EDITOR   Margaret Dornfeld
EDITORIAL ASSISTANT   Annie McDonnell
SENIOR DESIGNER   Rae Grant
PICTURE RESEARCHER   Lisa Kirchner
COVER ILLUSTRATOR   Daniel O'Leary

Copyright © 1994 by Chelsea House Publishers, a division of Main Line Book Co. All rights reserved.

Printed and bound in Mexico.

First Printing

1 3 5 7 9 8 6 4 2

Library of Congress Cataloging-in-Publication Data

Schwarz, Melissa.
  Wilma Mankiller : principal chief of the Cherokees / Melissa Schwarz : senior consulting editor, W. David Baird.
    p. cm. — (North American Indians of achievement)
  Includes bibliographical references and index.
  0-7910-1715-X
  1. Mankiller, Wilma Pearl, 1945– —Juvenile literature. 2. Cherokee Indians—Biography—Juvenile literature. 3. Cherokee Indians—Politics and government—Juvenile literature. 4. Indians of North America—Government relations—1934– —Juvenile literature. I. Baird, W. David. II. Title. III. Series.
E99.C5M3364 1994   93-44435
973'.04975'0092—dc20   CIP
  [B]   AC

CONTENTS

On Indian Leadership
W. David Baird   7

1   Indian Rights   11
2   One of the Principal People   23
3   A New Life   39
4   Awakening   51
5   Being of Good Mind   61
6   Building Unity and Independence   73
7   The Campaign   85
8   The Life of a Principal Chief   97

Chronology   107
Further Reading   108
Index   109

NORTH AMERICAN INDIANS OF ACHIEVEMENT

BLACK HAWK
Sac Rebel

JOSEPH BRANT
Mohawk Chief

BEN NIGHTHORSE CAMPBELL
Cheyenne Chief
and U.S. Senator

COCHISE
Apache Chief

CRAZY HORSE
Sioux War Chief

CHIEF GALL
Sioux War Chief

GERONIMO
Apache Warrior

HIAWATHA
Founder of the
Iroquois Confederacy

CHIEF JOSEPH
Nez Perce Leader

PETER MACDONALD
Former Chairman of
the Navajo Nation

WILMA MANKILLER
Principal Chief of the Cherokees

OSCEOLA
Seminole Rebel

QUANAH PARKER
Comanche Chief

KING PHILIP
Wampanoag Rebel

POCAHONTAS
Powhatan Peacemaker

PONTIAC
Ottawa Rebel

RED CLOUD
Sioux War Chief

WILL ROGERS
Cherokee Entertainer

SITTING BULL
Chief of the Sioux

TECUMSEH
Shawnee Rebel

JIM THORPE
Sac and Fox Athlete

SARAH WINNEMUCCA
Northern Paiute Writer and Diplomat

Other titles in preparation

On Indian Leadership

by W. David Baird
Howard A. White Professor of History
Pepperdine University

"Authoritative utterance is in thy mouth, perception is in thy heart, and thy tongue is the shrine of justice," the ancient Egyptians said of their king. From him, the Egyptians expected authority, discretion, and just behavior. Homer's *Iliad* suggests that the Greeks demanded somewhat different qualities from their leaders: justice and judgment, wisdom and counsel, shrewdness and cunning, valor and action. It is not surprising that different people living at different times should seek different qualities from the individuals they looked to for guidance. By and large, a people's requirements for leadership are determined by two factors: their culture and the unique circumstances of the time and place in which they live.

Before the late 15th century, when non-Indians first journeyed to what is now North America, most Indian tribes were not ruled by a single person. Instead, there were village chiefs, clan headmen, peace chiefs, war chiefs, and a host of other types of leaders, each with his or her own specific duties. These influential people not only decided political matters but also helped shape their tribe's social, cultural, and religious life. Usually, Indian leaders held their positions because they had won the respect of their peers. Indeed, if a leader's followers at any time decided that he or she was out of step with the will of the people, they felt free to look to someone else for advice and direction.

Thus, the greatest achievers in traditional Indian communities were men and women of extraordinary talent. They were not only skilled at navigating the deadly waters of tribal politics and cultural customs but also able to, directly or indirectly, make a positive and significant difference in the daily life of their followers.

Introduction

From the beginning of their interaction with Native Americans, non-Indians failed to understand these features of Indian leadership. Early European explorers and settlers merely assumed that Indians had the same relationship with their leaders as non-Indians had with their kings and queens. European monarchs generally inherited their positions and ruled large nations however they chose, often with little regard for the desires or needs of their subjects. As a result, the settlers of Jamestown saw Pocahontas as a "princess" and Pilgrims dubbed Wampanoag leader Metacom "King Philip," envisioning them in roles very different from those in which their own people placed them.

As more and more non-Indians flocked to North America, the nature of Indian leadership gradually began to change. Influential Indians no longer had to take on the often considerable burden of pleasing only their own people; they also had to develop a strategy of dealing with the non-Indian newcomers. In a rapidly changing world, new types of Indian role models with new ideas and talents continually emerged. Some were warriors; others were peacemakers. Some held political positions within their tribes; others were writers, artists, religious prophets, or athletes. Although the demands of Indian leadership altered from generation to generation, several factors that determined which Indian people became prominent in the centuries after first contact remained the same.

Certain personal characteristics distinguished these Indians of achievement. They were intelligent, imaginative, practical, daring, shrewd, uncompromising, ruthless, and logical. They were constant in friendships, unrelenting in hatreds, affectionate with their relatives, and respectful to their God or gods. Of course, no single Native American leader embodied all these qualities, nor these qualities only. But it was these characteristics that allowed them to succeed.

The special skills and talents that certain Indians possessed also brought them to positions of importance. The life of Hiawatha, the legendary founder of the powerful Iroquois Confederacy, displays the value that oratorical ability had for many Indians in power.

Introduction

The biography of Cochise, the 19th-century Apache chief, illustrates that leadership often required keen diplomatic skills not only in transactions among tribespeople but also in hardheaded negotiations with non-Indians. For others, such as Mohawk Joseph Brant and Navajo Peter MacDonald, a non-Indian education proved advantageous in their dealings with other peoples.

Sudden changes in circumstance were another crucial factor in determining who became influential in Indian communities. King Philip in the 1670s and Geronimo in the 1880s both came to power when their people were searching for someone to lead them into battle against white frontiersmen who had forced upon them a long series of indignities. Seeing the rising discontent of Indians of many tribes in the 1810s, Tecumseh and his brother, the Shawnee prophet Tenskwatawa, proclaimed a message of cultural revitalization that appealed to thousands. Other Indian achievers recognized cooperation with non-Indians as the most advantageous path during their lifetime. Sarah Winnemucca in the late 19th century bridged the gap of understanding between her people and their non-Indian neighbors through the publication of her autobiography *Life Among the Piutes*. Olympian Jim Thorpe in the early 20th century championed the assimilationist policies of the U.S. government and, with his own successes, demonstrated the accomplishments Indians could make in the non-Indian world. And Wilma Mankiller, principal chief of the Cherokees, continues to fight successfully for the rights of her people through the courts and through negotiation with federal officials.

Leadership among Native Americans, just as among all other peoples, can be understood only in the context of culture and history. But the centuries that Indians have had to cope with invasions of foreigners in their homelands have brought unique hardships and obstacles to the Native American individuals who most influenced and inspired others. Despite these challenges, there has never been a lack of Indian men and women equal to these tasks. With such strong leaders, it is no wonder that Native Americans remain such a vital part of this nation's cultural landscape.

1

INDIAN RIGHTS

In the early hours of November 20, 1969, 89 Native American men, women, and children boarded a small fleet of private boats, stole across San Francisco Bay, and seized the federally owned island of Alcatraz. Declaring the island Indian property, they set out to remind the nation not only of the vast expanses of land that the U.S. government had taken from their ancestors but also of the manipulation, discrimination, and oppression Indians continued to face as they tried to move toward the future. For citizens in San Francisco and across the country, the Alcatraz protest was a startling challenge to government authority. For Wilma Mankiller, it was an inspiration.

In 1969, at the age of 24, Mankiller led a quiet, comfortable life with her husband, Hugo Olaya, and her two small daughters. The family lived in a spacious home in a pretty San Francisco neighborhood, and Mankiller spent most of her days keeping house and caring for her children. Olaya, an immigrant from Ecuador, was an accountant and earned enough to support the household. Before their wedding, in 1963, the couple had agreed that when their first child was born, Mankiller would stop working and stay home to care for the family.

Mankiller enjoyed family life, but after the first few years of her marriage, she had begun to feel restless. Living in San Francisco in the 1960s, she was surrounded

Indian protesters celebrate the occupation of Alcatraz Island with a Thanksgiving feast on November 27, 1969. The meal was prepared by a San Francisco restaurant and delivered to the island by Sausalito yachtsmen.

by artists, students, activists, and individualists calling for freedom and change. All around her, people were experimenting with new ideas and new ways of living, and she sensed that if she could become part of what was happening, she might affect society more deeply than she did in her activities as a mother and a wife. But it was not until she heard the news of the Alcatraz takeover that she began to realize what kind of role she wanted to play.

The rocky shores of Alcatraz Island had once been a stopping place for the Ohlones, a local Indian tribe. The Indians were driven from the area by the Spanish in the late 1700s, and from that time on, Alcatraz had been in the hands of white officials. By the 1870s, the U.S. Army had taken over the island and built a military prison there, and in 1933, its cells were transformed into a high-security federal penitentiary. After the prison was closed down in 1963, Indian political groups asked the U.S. government to return the island to the Native American community, but their request was denied. Finally, on the night of November 9, 1969, a group of 14 Native Americans, most of them college students, caught

From 1933 to 1963, Alcatraz Island was the site of a high-security federal penitentiary. This photograph was taken the year before the prison closed.

a ride on a charter boat headed for Alcatraz and claimed the island "in the name of Indians of All Tribes." The students gave up their claim after 19 hours, but 10 days later they were followed by a much larger band of demonstrators, this one determined to stay until the U.S. government responded to their demands.

Many of the Indians involved in the occupation hoped the United States could really be persuaded to surrender Alcatraz. In general, however, the takeover was intended not so much to recover a piece of land as to draw attention to the abuses Indians had suffered in the past and continued to endure as American citizens. Over the past two centuries of U.S.–Indian relations, the U.S. Army, government officials, and white settlers had taken millions of acres of land from Indian tribes. Thousands of Indians had died in defense of these lands; thousands more had succumbed to diseases brought by European settlers. Now, nearly 100 years after the last Indian war, Native Americans were still struggling to recover. According to a well-publicized study, in the late 1960s, three-quarters of the Indian population was living in poverty; Native Americans were among the poorest minority groups in the country. More than 40 percent were unemployed, and on the average almost half dropped out of school before graduating. Health problems among Indian groups had become so serious that most Indians died while they were still in their forties, although the average American lived to be nearly 70 years old.

Wilma Mankiller knew many of these problems firsthand. Her own father was a full-blooded Cherokee, and her ancestors had been betrayed many times by the U.S. government. In 1838, the Cherokees had been driven from their homelands—an area that stretched from present-day Virginia south to Alabama—and forced to walk 1,200 miles to a section of land west of the Mississippi River known then as Indian Territory. U.S.

officials had signed a treaty promising the Indians that their new land would belong to them forever. But in the early 1900s, Congress passed a number of laws that gradually took the Cherokees' sovereignty away from them. By 1907, when Indian Territory became the state of Oklahoma, much of the tribe's land had been given to white settlers.

By the mid-1950s, most of those Cherokees who still lived in Oklahoma were so poor they could hardly survive. The Mankiller family was no exception. In 1956, when Wilma was 11, the Bureau of Indian Affairs (BIA) helped the Mankillers leave their farm in Oklahoma and move to San Francisco, where Wilma's father hoped to find work. The family's decision to move was influenced by a new government policy known as termination. U.S. officials at that time believed that if they encouraged Indians to become self-sufficient, eventually the government would be able to "terminate" the tribe and stop giving them financial assistance. The BIA was pursuing this policy by moving Indian families into cities where, officials hoped, they would blend into mainstream America.

BIA agents had gone to Indian communities such as the Mankillers' in Oklahoma and handed out brochures promising that "good jobs," "happy homes," and an "exciting community life" awaited Indians who accepted the government's offer of relocation. But those cheery words were very different from the reality that awaited the Mankillers. They arrived in San Francisco only to find that well-paying jobs were almost as hard to come by there as they had been in Oklahoma. The only apartment they could afford was in a neighborhood where it was dangerous for the children to play outdoors. For the Mankillers and other Indian families who had believed the false assurances of the BIA, it was yet another deception in a long history of broken promises.

Fighting discrimination, isolation, and the many problems that came with urban life, the Mankillers gradually built a better life for themselves. By working long hours, Wilma's father earned enough to support his large family, eventually becoming a shop steward and a union leader with a spice company based in San Francisco. Wilma herself finished high school and attended college—something neither of her parents had been able to do.

As time passed, the Mankiller family became friends with other Indians who had come to the city under the BIA program. These Indians were from all over the country and belonged to many different tribes, but as they shared their frustrations over the relocation policy, their tribal differences faded. More and more they turned to each other, rather than to federal agents, for support. By the early 1960s, Indians in San Francisco and other cities were organizing community projects aimed at reviving Native American culture and improving the lives of urban Indian families. The Mankillers took part in many of these projects. They attended powwows in Golden Gate Park, singing and dancing with other Indians and sharing Indian foods, and spent much of their free time at a community-run organization called the San Francisco Indian Center, socializing and discussing politics with their Indian friends.

During this same period, the civil rights movement was changing the way the nation thought about race and the rights of minorities. Slowly, it was giving urban Indians a sense of empowerment. In 1968, a group of Indians in Minneapolis, Minnesota, started the American Indian Movement (AIM), a political association whose goals were to make the U.S. government fulfill its treaty obligations and give more support to impoverished Indian families. This organization soon had branches in cities all over the country; its San Francisco chapter helped launch the attack on Alcatraz.

Wilma Mankiller was deeply attached to her Indian heritage and profoundly aware of the sad history of U.S.–Indian relations. Still, in 1969, she was not a political activist; she had joined neither the American Indian Movement nor its neighbor organization in San Francisco, United Native Americans, Inc. With the action at Alcatraz—a demonstration that demanded Indian rights with urgency and power—her life began to change. Soon after she heard the news of the takeover, she began to meet regularly with other Native Americans at the San Francisco Indian Center. As she discussed the protest with her friends and acquaintances at the center, she found that the majority were as excited about the occupation as she was. Though some people worried that the takeover would turn federal authorities against Native Americans, most expressed feelings of pride and satisfaction at the protest. Their ancestors had lost millions of acres of land to U.S. authorities. Now, at last, the Indians on Alcatraz had taken something back.

The Indians who had seized the island soon sent out a proclamation explaining the purpose of the protest. Adopting a tone of sharp irony, the document pointed out the mistreatment Indians had suffered ever since their first contact with Europeans. The Indians on Alcatraz, according to the proclamation, wanted to be "fair and honorable in [their] dealings with the Caucasian inhabitants" of the island, and were prepared to pay them "$24 in glass beads and red cloth [for the land], a precedent set by the white man's purchase of a similar island about 300 years ago." This was a stinging reference to the paltry price European settlers had paid for the island of Manhattan in New York City in one of the most outrageous land treaties in Indian history. But such exploitative practices, the document made clear, were by no means a thing of the past. Since Alcatraz Island consisted of 16 acres of land, the Indians' offer amounted to $1.24 an acre. This was more than twice the 47 cents an acre that the federal government was currently offering California's Pit River tribe for land that had been taken from them in the 1800s.

Commenting on the condition of Indian reservations, the proclamation continued:

> We feel that this . . . island is more than suitable as an Indian Reservation, as determined by the white man's own standards. By this we mean that this place resembles most Indian reservations, in that:
>
> 1. It is isolated from modern facilities, and without adequate means of transportation.
> 2. It has no fresh running water.
> 3. The sanitation facilities are inadequate.
> 4. There are no oil or mineral rights.
> 5. There is no industry and so unemployment is very great.
> 6. There are no health care facilities.
> 7. The soil is rocky and non-productive and the land does not support game.
> 8. There are no educational facilities.
> 9. The population has always been held as prisoners and kept dependent on others.

The proclamation, which went on to describe the Indian cultural center the protesters hoped to build on the island, was signed "INDIANS OF ALL TRIBES, November 1969, San Francisco, CA."

As the occupation continued, Wilma Mankiller became more and more involved in the movement that supported it. Many Indians, including four of Mankiller's siblings, eventually traveled to Alcatraz to take part in the occupation. Mankiller herself visited the island, but for the most part she chose to stay on the mainland, where she helped raise funds and did other work to keep the protest alive.

There was plenty of work for everyone. The people on

Alcatraz needed a steady supply of food, water, blankets, and other goods. The delivery of these necessities was complicated, as the island was accessible only by boat. Fortunately, many people who lived in the cities around San Francisco Bay, non-Indians as well as Indians, supported the takeover and were willing to donate money, clothes, and transportation.

For the first few days of the takeover, the California Coast Guard set up a blockade around Alcatraz to keep supplies from getting to the island. Each day a few boats managed to evade the Coast Guard ships. The blockade made such a dramatic story that it kept Alcatraz and the Indians' cause on the front page of American newspapers for an entire week. Public support for the Indians was so strong that after three days the Coast Guard gave up.

Exhilarated by their success, the Indians planned a special victory celebration to take place on November 27, 1969, Thanksgiving Day. Volunteers on the mainland organized a fleet of private boats from around the bay so that they could travel to "Indian land" and take part in the event. Bratskellers, a San Francisco restaurant, donated a lavish turkey dinner for everyone to enjoy.

On the afternoon of November 27, more than 500 Indians gathered in the main recreation yard of the abandoned prison. The high cement walls, still topped with rusting barbed wire, protected them from the strong, cold winds blowing across San Francisco Bay. One of the protest leaders, Adam Fortunate Eagle, later described the scene in his book, *Alcatraz! Alcatraz!*:

> A few years before my Aunt Anna had given me my great-uncle's ceremonial pipe, and I brought it out on this historic day. . . . It was a beautiful and meaningful moment when the pipe passed among so many different Indian people. We were people from all four directions; our tribes came from the north and the south, the east and the west coasts. There was a hushed awe and respect among the

A young activist paints a sign on a federal prison building on Alcatraz. Soon after occupying the island, Indian demonstrators issued a proclamation offering to compensate the government for the property, which they hoped to use as a cultural center.

crowd, for it is our tradition that as the pipe is passed one must be of good heart, mind, and body. One must release all negative thoughts such as anger or hate, or those thoughts will come back on oneself. I watched as young and old smoked. The island warriors, to whom we owed so much for physically risking themselves in the fight to take and hold the island, smoked and passed the pipe to those who were supporting their effort from the mainland. It was truly a united effort and we were truly Indians of all tribes.

When the boat containing the Thanksgiving dinner arrived, volunteers set up long tables for the food. There was turkey with cranberry sauce, sweet potatoes, and cake from the restaurant, plus home-cooked stews and Indian dishes that supporters had brought from home. While hungry sea gulls circled above them, visitors filled their plates and sat on the concrete steps of the main cell block to enjoy the feast.

The Indian occupation of Alcatraz lasted 19 months. During that time, an organization called United Bay Area Council of American Indian Affairs, Inc., was formed to negotiate with government officials for the island. Most people in the Bay Area wanted to give the island to the Indians; after all, they noted, it was not being used for anything else. But government officials were afraid that if they agreed, the Indians' success would lead to similar takeovers all over the country. So much land had been taken from the Indians that, as one California senator put it, "if Indians are successful in claiming Alcatraz, somebody's liable to claim the whole United States."

The protesters were eventually forced to leave the island, but in a sense their demonstration was a success. For more than a year and a half, they made the nation listen to their demands for fair treatment. During the occupation of Alcatraz, more than 13,000 Indians came to visit the island. They left with a renewed sense of pride in their culture. For Indians around the country, Alcatraz became a symbol of hope.

At the time, Indian groups in Washington, D.C., such as the National Indian Youth Council, were working hard for change. These groups had been telling the federal government that their people did not want to be told how to live by the Bureau of Indian Affairs. They wanted the financial assistance they had coming to them, but they wanted to use it in whatever way they saw fit. Put simply, Native Americans wanted control of their own lives.

The termination policy of the 1950s had been designed to make Indians more self-sufficient so the government could stop giving them aid. It did so by encouraging them to reject their traditional culture and enter mainstream American society. The occupation of Alcatraz demonstrated that Indians were determined to change this policy.

In an address to Congress on July 8, 1971, two months after the Alcatraz protest ended, President Richard Nixon admitted that American Indians had become "the most deprived and isolated minority group in our nation." He went on to declare: "It is time we recognized the enormous contributions Indians have made to the country's art and culture, to its strength and spirit, to its sense of history and its sense of purpose."

Nixon acknowledged that the government had no right to terminate its care-giving relationship with the Indians "as though it had been entered into as an act of generosity, instead of through treaties that represented the U.S. government's commitments in exchange for vast tracts of land." He continued, "We must begin to act on the basis of what the Indians themselves have long been calling for, a new era in which the Indian future is determined by Indian acts and Indian decisions." Announcing a new federal Indian policy called self-determination, Nixon promised that the government would now try to "strengthen the Indian's sense of autonomy without threatening his sense of community."

Hearing the president of the United States accept what Indians had been saying for so long, Wilma Mankiller, along with many other Indians around the country, saw that the invasion of Alcatraz had indeed brought progress. Still, she knew that real change would take time. In 1971, Mankiller had barely begun her work to promote Indian rights; in the years to come, as Indians everywhere continued to fight for self-determination and a better standard of living, she would become one of their most prominent leaders.

2
ONE OF THE PRINCIPAL PEOPLE

Wilma Pearl Mankiller was born on November 18, 1945, in a small Indian hospital a few minutes from her family's farm outside Rocky Mountain, Oklahoma. Her mother, Irene, came from a Dutch-Irish family that arrived in America in the 1800s. Her father, Charley, was a full-blooded Cherokee. This made Wilma Mankiller a "mixed-blood" Cherokee, but the fact that her mother was not Indian was to have little bearing on her life. Charley Mankiller identified strongly with his tribe, and although he encouraged his daughter to learn the ways of non-Indian society, he raised her as a Cherokee.

When Charley Mankiller was growing up, the Oklahoma Cherokees were becoming poorer; more and more of them were coming to depend on federal aid for their survival. By the time Wilma Mankiller was born, every aspect of Cherokee life—education, health care, living conditions, and employment—had deteriorated.

The Mankillers lived in a small wooden house that Wilma's father had built himself. "I remember it as a

Wilma Mankiller (front row, right) gathers with six of her siblings near their home at Mankiller Flats, Oklahoma, in 1949.

little bitty house with too many people living there," Mankiller wrote later. "[It] had four rooms, all with bare plank floors and walls. It was covered by a tin roof. In the winter, our only heat came from a wood stove. That is also how we cooked. There was no electricity, and we used coal-oil lamps to light the rooms. We had a few pieces of furniture. There was an outhouse for a toilet."

Charley and Irene Mankiller already had five children when Wilma was born, and in the years to come they would have five more. Taking care of a big family is difficult under any circumstances, but for the Mankillers it meant constant work. Though Charley had inherited his father's land, known as Mankiller Flats, the soil there was poor. It took long hours of work each day just to produce enough food to feed the family. Wilma's mother canned jars of tomatoes, beans, and corn from the family vegetable garden and harvested wild onions, mushrooms, and berries from the nearby woods. Wilma's father and brothers hunted and fished. To cover their other expenses, the Mankillers sold strawberries, green beans, peanuts, and timber. Some of the children's clothing was made from flour sacks, which came in a rough cotton fabric printed with floral designs.

It was a hard life, but for Wilma it was not an unhappy one. Wilma Mankiller grew up with a clear sense that money was not the most important value in life. Although her family worked hard and had few possessions, she would later feel that she had been fortunate, for she and her brothers and sisters were raised in an atmosphere of love and support.

Wilma was a curious, independent child with a strong will, and she grew up quickly. When she was old enough, she helped her older brothers and sisters with chores around the farm. There was always something to do: cooking, cleaning, washing, sewing, working in the garden, watching new babies, or hauling water from the stream a quarter-mile away.

As often as not, Wilma found these jobs tiresome. "I lingered and dawdled," she wrote later. "I spent much more time trying to figure out how to avoid chores than it would have taken to do them." What she really loved was exploring the hills surrounding her family's farm. Mankiller Flats may not have brought in much money, but to a young Cherokee girl it was a beautiful place. She made up games, raced through the quiet forests of oak, sycamore, and dogwood, and became familiar with deer, foxes, snakes, and other animals that lived in the area.

There were toys to play with, too—jump ropes, jacks, and Chinese checkers—and books to read. Charley Mankiller loved books, and he passed this passion on to his children. Wilma would one day regard her enthusiasm for reading as one of the most valuable gifts her family ever gave her. The pleasure the Mankillers found in this pastime, she would decide, was a natural extension of the Cherokee tradition of telling and listening to stories.

Storytelling was a part of daily life in the Mankiller household. In the evening, after all the chores were done, the family would sit together, the older children on the floor and the youngest in their parents' laps. Wilma knew that the stories told at this time had been passed down for generations, and she loved to hear them. She always asked questions, and before long she knew much of the tribe's history by heart.

Wilma learned that her family name, *Mankiller*, came from a military rank given to an ancestor who was a warrior chief in the mid-1700s. The Cherokees' name in their own language was *Ani'Yun'wiya*, which means "the principal people." The tribe had existed for more than 1,000 years before Europeans came to the Americas. She also learned that before the Cherokees came to Oklahoma,

Wilma's father, Charley Mankiller, sits on his father's knee in an early 20th-century family portrait.

they had lived in a land of mountains, green valleys, forests, and rivers. This territory later became the states of Tennessee, Virginia, West Virginia, South Carolina, and Kentucky, and parts of Georgia, Alabama, and North Carolina.

The Cherokee people had lived differently then, in villages that stretched for miles along the banks of rivers. The hills around these communities abounded with deer and other animals for Cherokee men to hunt. Wilma Mankiller's father explained that in the past, every Cherokee Indian belonged to a clan, which was like a big family. There were seven clans: Wolf, Deer, Bird, Paint, Long Hair, Blue, and Wild Potato. Cherokee villages were run by councils that included members of each group. Other tribes—the Creeks and the Choctaws, for example—lived in nearby territories, and Cherokee warriors occasionally went to war against them. Sometimes Cherokee women fought too.

One such woman, Nancy Ward, a member of the Wolf clan, became well known for her fighting skills. At some point early in her life, she accompanied her husband, a warrior named Kingfisher, on a campaign against the Creeks. Kingfisher was killed during the battle, but Nancy Ward, instead of fleeing in grief, picked up her husband's gun and led the rest of the Cherokee warriors to victory. Wilma Mankiller heard the story of Nancy Ward many times while she was growing up, and the legend helped her to realize that Cherokee women were just as strong as Cherokee men.

When the first Europeans arrived in Cherokee villages, the principal people observed that the newcomers were very different from themselves. The Cherokees traded with them, exchanging deer skins for knives and metal tools, but for the most part, they kept the foreigners at a distance. In time, however, many Cherokees died from smallpox, bubonic plague, and other European diseases that had never before existed in the Americas. Before long, there were fewer Cherokees than settlers living in the Cherokee homeland. Not only did the settlers want Indian land for themselves, Wilma Mankiller's relatives explained to her, but they wanted the Indians to change and become more like them. By the time the United States had become an independent nation, near the end of the 18th century, the Cherokees felt they had only two choices: to accept non-Indian ways or to fight.

Most of the Cherokees soon decided it would be better to adopt non-Indian customs; they may have hoped that if they changed and became more like whites, the settlers would allow them to live in peace in their homeland. The U.S. government sent agents to teach the Indians the ways of American society. With the help of Christian missionaries, the Cherokees built schools and churches and learned to read and write English. The men stopped hunting and started to plant crops. Cherokee women, who once cultivated their families' food, began to spin yarn and weave cloth as non-Indian women did. Soon, the Cherokee way of life so closely resembled non-Indian society that the Cherokees and four neighboring tribes—the Creeks, Choctaws, Chickasaws, and Seminoles—became known to the whites as the Five Civilized Tribes.

Despite their willingness to adapt, the Cherokees did not allow the settlers to dominate them. In 1819, even as most Cherokees were becoming proficient in English, a brilliant Cherokee man named Sequoyah invented an alphabet for the Cherokee language, and within six months, most tribe members could read and write

Sequoyah, inventor of the Cherokee alphabet, displays his work in 1819. Using Sequoyah's alphabet, most Cherokees learned to read and write in their own language; in 1828, they established the Cherokee Phoenix, a bilingual newspaper.

This 19th-century portrait shows John Ross, the first principal chief of the Cherokee Nation, beside his wife, Mary Bryan Stapler Ross. Under Ross's leadership, the tribe created the Cherokee Constitution, a governing document modeled on the Constitution of the United States.

Cherokee. One of the more affluent members of the tribe bought a printing press, and the Cherokees created their own bilingual newspaper. Meanwhile, many Cherokee families flourished under the white farming system; some became wealthy plantation owners.

As the years passed, the way the Cherokee people governed themselves changed too. As the government in Washington, D.C., pushed them to sign more treaties, it became clear to the Cherokees that they could negotiate more successfully if they had strong leaders to defend their interests. Instead of relying on village councils for leadership, the Cherokees began to elect leaders—a principal chief, an assistant chief, and other officials—in much the same way white citizens elected the president of the United States. The role of these leaders was to govern the entire Cherokee tribe, and their republic came to be known as the Cherokee Nation. In 1827, under Chief John Ross, the Cherokees wrote their own constitution, a book of laws modeled on the U.S. Constitution.

When American citizens heard about the Cherokee Constitution, many of them grew alarmed. They had encouraged the Cherokees to learn new ways, but they had not intended the Indians to use what they learned to create legal documents. They worried that the constitution would help the Cherokees defend their claim to their traditional territory. Instead of welcoming this Cherokee effort to embrace U.S.–style democracy, politicians in the state of Georgia declared the Cherokee Constitution illegal.

At the same time, rumors were spreading that there was gold in Cherokee territory. Prospectors poured in from everywhere, tearing down the Indians' fences and destroying their crops. The state of Georgia, which claimed jurisdiction over Cherokee territory, supported such encroachments by making it illegal for an Indian to bring suit or testify against a white man in court.

Appealing to President Andrew Jackson, the Cherokees pointed out that the American government had signed treaties with them, guaranteeing their right to the land. But Jackson, a seasoned Indian fighter, claimed that there was little the federal government could do to control the state of Georgia.

In 1830, the U.S. Congress passed the Indian Removal Act. This new law gave Jackson the authority to buy all the land east of the Mississippi River that belonged to the Five Civilized Tribes. In return, the American government would offer the Indians a section of land west of the Mississippi, in what is now the state of Oklahoma.

Officials in Washington convinced the Creeks, Choctaws, Chickasaws, and Seminoles that moving west was in their best interest, but the Cherokees could not be persuaded to move. Finally, federal land agents threatened to use force if the tribe did not leave their land within two years.

A few Cherokees who were disgusted with the situation left immediately, but the majority were determined to stay. They believed that they could change the government's policy by negotiating. They were wrong. In the summer of 1838, federal troops entered Cherokee territory and placed the entire tribe under arrest. Children were separated from parents as hundreds of Indians were locked in stockades, where they were deprived of adequate food and water. The captive Indians could only watch in horror as troops burned their cabins and crops so they would have nothing to return to. To prevent his people from starving, Chief Ross finally gave in. He told U.S. officials he would sell the tribe's territory if they would allow the Cherokees to move west on their own.

A number of Cherokees opposed Ross's agreement, and that summer, a small group of them fled and hid in the Tennessee mountains. The following winter, the remainder of the tribe—about 18,000 people—traveled some 1,200 miles to Indian Territory. Some went by horse, and a few others rode in wagons, but most of the tribe was forced to make the hard journey on foot. More than 4,000 Cherokees died from disease or exposure to the cold and were buried along the way. This tragic phase of Cherokee history later became known as the Trail of Tears.

Wilma Mankiller heard the story of the Trail of Tears often while she was growing up. Her father's great-grandparents had been part of the exodus to Indian Territory, and one of her aunts owned a cooking utensil that had been transported all the way from the Cherokee homeland.

Cherokee schoolboys line up to mark a section of the Trail of Tears for Grant Foreman, a historian who traced the path of the tribe in the early 1930s.

As terrible as this time of hardship was, Mankiller knew that the Cherokee people had not allowed it to destroy their spirit. The Cherokees had given up their original homeland in exchange for some 4 million acres in Indian Territory and the right to control this land independently of any other government. They were determined to make the best of it. Under their own tribal government, they built schools and hospitals in their new location and established a criminal justice system in accordance with the Cherokee Constitution.

For the most part, the Cherokees continued to live according to non-Indian ways, but they also retained certain traditions that set them apart. Following ancient

Announcing the opening of Indian Territory to white settlement, an 1897 broadside claims that "the Indians are rejoicing to have the whites settle up this country." The advertised land was purchased from the Creek, Seminole, Chickasaw, and Chocktaw tribes, but as more settlers moved into the region they began to take land still owned by the Cherokees.

custom, the Cherokee Nation remained the official owner of all the tribe's land; individual Cherokees did not own separate lots but could use as much of the land as they needed. This arrangement worked well for Wilma's ancestors. Only five decades before Wilma Mankiller was born, most Cherokees were making a good living running their own farms or ranches, or mining for coal or gold. A few were even quite wealthy, and Cherokees who did not want to run their own farms could often find jobs working for those who did.

However, as the United States grew, settlers began moving west into Indian Territory. Although officially the land belonged to the Indians, the Cherokee Nation, whose legal powers were limited, had no way of preventing the newcomers from settling on it. The Cherokees tried to live with the settlers in peace, but as the non-Indian population grew, so too did tensions between the two communities. The Cherokee Nation appealed to the United States for help, but it got little response from the government.

By 1890, there were once again more non-Indians in Cherokee territory than there were Cherokees, and the settlers had become a powerful political group. They began to pressure the U.S. government to take back some of the Indians' land and make their own land claims legal. At the same time, officials in Washington were beginning to change their views on the Cherokee practice of holding land in common. They argued that if Indian families owned separate plots of land, as white people did, they would be more likely to assimilate into American society. They decided to break up the tribal government and divide the land among Indians and non-Indians.

Wilma Mankiller's great-grandparents and other Cherokees of their generation fought this decision in court for many years, but ultimately federal officials forced them to accept the policy. Starting in 1902, land controlled by the Cherokee Nation was divided into allotments. The head of each Cherokee family was given an allotment of 160 acres; it was in this way that Wilma's grandfather, John Mankiller, came to own Mankiller Flats. All the Cherokees who were awarded land were made citizens of the United States. The rest of the Cherokee land was given to non-Indian homesteaders. When Oklahoma became a state in 1907, Indian Territory ceased to exist and the Cherokee Nation was dissolved.

What followed was an era of Cherokee history Wilma

Cherokees gather for a meal of chicken and beans in Elm Springs, Oklahoma.

Mankiller would later call "a long period of decline." After the allotment law was passed, those who had been ranchers or miners were forced to try to make their living by farming. Many of the allotments—including Mankiller Flats—consisted of land that was too rocky and dry to farm, and the Indians did not have enough money to dig wells or build irrigation systems. Nor could most of them buy farm equipment or livestock. In the past, they had relied on the Cherokee Nation when they needed assistance, but under the new system, they were forced to scrape by on their own.

Wilma knew that her tribe had gone through many hard times; she was also aware that despite their troubled history the Cherokees had managed to keep much of their culture alive. Most of the people she knew during her childhood in Oklahoma had grown up speaking the Cherokee language. Her own family used both English and Cherokee, and sometimes they mixed the two. Her mother learned to speak Cherokee fairly well, even though the language was not a part of her background.

Wilma was most aware of the Cherokee spirit when her parents took her to the Stomp Ground, a special place where ceremonial dances were held. These tribal events would remain some of her happiest memories. "I remember all the food and people," she later wrote. "There were always lots of children to run and play with, and laughter, and no set bedtime for anyone." At the Stomp Ground, Wilma would watch as her father and other Cherokee men danced around a huge fire. The fire was deeply symbolic; it was lit from a flame that generations of Cherokees had kept burning for hundreds of years. It had burned before Europeans came to Cherokee country, and it had continued to burn when the Indians formed the Cherokee Nation. An ember from that sacred fire had been carried from the Cherokee homeland all the way to Indian Territory on the Trail of Tears.

Another Cherokee tradition Wilma took part in was a game called stickball. Like the tribal dances, this pastime had belonged to Cherokee culture for centuries, and there were several ways of playing it. In one version, the players spread out over an open field, at the center of which was a long pole supporting a wooden fish that could spin around like a weather vane. There were two teams of men and women. While the men carried two wooden sticks, each with a small net attached to one end, the women played only with their hands. The object of the game was to catch the ball, then hurl it at the fish and make it spin. Each time someone hit the fish, he or she received points. Stickball was an aggressive game, and sometimes people were injured. Wilma was told that in earlier days, the Cherokees would sometimes settle disputes with other tribes by playing stickball, instead of going to war.

When Wilma Mankiller was six, she started attending Rocky Mountain Elementary School. At this small, white building three miles from her home, Wilma learned reading, writing, geography, and other basic subjects. She also learned for the first time that not everyone lived as she did. She noticed that her teachers spoke and dressed differently from the people in her community. In her 1993 autobiography, *Mankiller: A Chief and Her People,* she writes: "I didn't know the difference between being poor and having money until one day at school. A little girl whose family had more than most of us saw my flour-sack underwear while we were in the outhouse. She ran and told some other girls, and they all teased me about it. That was really the first time I had any inkling that we were different."

As she grew older, Wilma became even more aware of the gulf that separated her family from their wealthier neighbors, and she shied away from people who were not part of the Indian community. Much to her discomfort, she later wrote, strangers sometimes noticed Wilma and her sister walking to school and tried to treat them charitably:

> Some well-dressed white ladies occasionally would drive up in their big cars. They came to bring us clothes and offer us rides to school. . . . One time when we got inside their car, those ladies looked at us with sad expressions and said, "Bless your little hearts." It was not the words that got to me, but the way they said them, along with the looks on their faces.

Even as a child, Wilma Mankiller knew that this was not the kind of help she and her family needed. Like the classmates who teased her, these women only made her feel, in an embarrassing way, that she was "different." It was not until years later that she would come to see this difference—a difference that included a rich heritage and a wide range of experience—as something positive.

3
A NEW LIFE

In 1956, a terrible drought struck Oklahoma and the Midwest. For weeks, the area received no rain, and that summer the stream that flowed near the Mankiller farm—the family's only source of water—slowed to a trickle. The Mankillers' crops withered and died. Living on the food they had preserved the previous year, they were able to get through the winter, but by the spring of 1957, their stores were nearly exhausted. The Mankillers planted seeds and watched the skies, hoping for rain. The drought continued. When it was clear that they would have no crops for a second year, Charley Mankiller rode into the town of Stilwell to ask for a loan from the Bureau of Indian Affairs.

The officials at the BIA, however, were not interested in helping Indians stay on their farms. In 1953, Congress had voted to adopt the policy known as termination, and government agencies were now being told they must urge Indians to assimilate into mainstream American society. Most officials in Washington agreed that the best way for agents to do this was to encourage Indians to move away from their rural communities and live in the city.

Wearing a borrowed buckskin dress, 17-year-old Wilma Mankiller (right) attends a powwow with a friend in the San Francisco Bay area in 1962.

Thus, when Charley Mankiller arrived at the Stilwell BIA office, he learned that there was no money available for a loan. Then a BIA official told him about the federal relocation program, making it sound very appealing. The official told Charley that if he moved his family to the city the BIA would help him find a good job and a comfortable apartment.

Charley Mankiller had lived at Mankiller Flats all his life, and he was very reluctant to leave. His brothers and sisters and their families lived nearby, and he knew that moving would be hard on his children. But he also knew that the family would not be able to survive much longer on the farm if the drought continued. If what the BIA officer said was true, living in the city would give his children educational opportunities that they did not have in rural Oklahoma. After talking the matter over for many days, Charley and Irene Mankiller decided to accept the BIA's offer. The agency offered them a choice of Chicago, Oakland, or San Francisco, and the Mankillers picked San Francisco, because Irene's mother lived about 90 miles away from there, in Riverbank, California.

To Wilma and her younger brothers and sisters, the thought of moving was terrifying. "None of us little kids could visualize California," she later recalled. "We had been as far as Muskogee to go to the fair on a school field trip, . . . but that was about it. [My sister and I] talked of running away to avoid the move, but we never did that. We kept hoping right up until the day our family left that something would happen—some kind of miracle—and we would stay put and not have to go."

The Mankillers sold off what they could not carry and packed the rest. Then, early one October morning, they climbed into a neighbor's car and rode to the Stilwell train station. Wilma Mankiller was just about to turn 11. "As we drove away, I looked at our house, the store, my school," she wrote later. "I took last looks. I wanted to remember it all. I tried to memorize the shapes of the trees, the calls of animals and birds from the forest. All of us looked out the windows. We did not want to forget anything."

As the family got under way, Charley and Irene Mankiller tried to appear confident and optimistic, but leaving Oklahoma was a sad experience for everyone. The younger children watched with trepidation as the California-bound locomotive rumbled into the railroad station. Having never seen a train before, they were only too happy to heed their parents' warning to stay close together.

The Mankillers spent the next two days crying, watching the changing landscape from the train windows, and trying not to worry about the future. When the train finally arrived at downtown San Francisco's crowded station, a BIA relocation officer met them and explained that the government would pay for a hotel until they could find an apartment. They would receive a weekly allowance for food and other necessities for four weeks or until Charley Mankiller got his first paycheck.

Wilma Mankiller never forgot her first few days in the city. "We didn't know what to expect," she later recalled. "No idea at all. The noise, the tall buildings, the sheer number of people—it was all overwhelming." The first night the family spent in San Francisco, Wilma thought she heard a wild animal screaming and went running to her parents. She and her younger siblings had never heard a siren before. "One day I was living in Oklahoma," she remembered. "And the next day I found myself in California, trying to deal with the mysteries of television, neon lights, and elevators. It was total culture shock."

The streets of San Francisco seemed so dangerous at

first that Charley Mankiller told his children to stay in the hotel room with their mother while he went out looking for a job. After a few days, however, the Mankillers began to adjust to city life. They learned to use a telephone and a toilet that flushed. They got used to walking on crowded streets where strangers passed each other without a word and stoplights controlled the flow of traffic.

The Mankillers moved into a small apartment in Potrero Hill, a poor neighborhood in San Francisco. Wilma's father and her oldest brother, Donald, found work in a rope factory, and Irene got the children started in school. But the family was still very poor, and in many ways, their life seemed harder than it had been in Oklahoma.

Like many relocated Indians, the Mankillers missed their home terribly. They missed the open spaces, the woods, and the bright stars in the night sky. Most of all, they missed their friends and the sense of community they had enjoyed in Oklahoma, where almost all their neighbors had been Cherokees. Very few Indian families lived in Potrero Hill.

Wilma felt especially out of place at school, where everyone immediately seemed to notice she was different. Every time her teacher called the roll, the other students would laugh at her name. *Mankiller* had not seemed like a strange name to the children at Rocky Mountain Elementary School, but to people in California it was very peculiar. Wilma's classmates also teased her about the way she talked and dressed. As the weeks wore on, she felt the only thing to do was make herself inconspicuous. It would be a long time before anything about her new home would appeal to her.

By the end of their first year in California, the Mankillers had saved enough money to move to a small house in Daly City, south of San Francisco. They had also begun to make friends with other Native Americans at the San Francisco Indian Center. These changes made life a little easier for most members of the family, but to Wilma they offered little comfort. At her new school in Daly City, she continued to feel stigmatized, and as she grew older her worries increased. "I was insecure, and the least little remark or glance would leave me morti-

Automobiles and cable cars ply San Francisco's busy Powell Street in the late 1950s. Moving from the quiet hills of rural Oklahoma to this city in 1957, the Mankillers were startled by the crowded spaces and bustling atmosphere of their new hometown.

fied," she wrote in her autobiography. "There were changes going on inside me that I could not account for, and that also troubled me.... I was experiencing all the problems girls face when approaching the beginning of womanhood . . . [and] I was growing like a weed. . . . I hated what was happening. I hated my body. I hated school. I hated the teachers. I hated the other students. Most of all, I hated the city."

As Wilma struggled to sort through her feelings, she felt there was no one to turn to for help. Her father was busy trying to support the family, and her mother had to divide her time among all the Mankiller children. Desperate to escape her situation, at the age of 12, Wilma decided to run away from home. Using money she had saved from baby-sitting, she bought a bus ticket and went to Riverbank, where her grandmother lived on a dairy farm near other families from Oklahoma. As soon as she arrived, her grandmother called her parents, and she was taken back to Daly City. But Wilma was determined to carry out her plan—the farm in Riverbank reminded her of home. Over the next year, she ran away to her grandmother five times. Finally, her parents agreed to let her stay on the farm for a whole year.

Wilma admired her grandmother, and through her example, she gradually learned to cope better with her troubles. Mankiller later described her grandmother as one of her most important role models:

> Although she was small, only about 4 feet 10 inches tall, she was solidly built. She was also opinionated, outspoken, tough, and very independent. She was deeply religious and sang from her hymnbook every day. . . . Even though she was strict, she was never judgmental. At a very critical point in my life, she helped me learn to accept myself and confront my problems.

Living on the farm meant hard work, but it was the kind of work Wilma was used to. She came to enjoy getting up with the sun to milk the cows, clean the stalls, and help her grandmother in the vegetable garden.

By the time Wilma returned to the Bay Area, her family had moved out of Daly City and into a rough San Francisco neighborhood called Hunter's Point. As the Mankillers settled in, they quickly learned about the many hazards that were a part of life in this district. Hunter's Point was riddled with crime. While the Mankillers tried to go on with their lives inside their small, two-story home, street gangs clashed outside their windows. According to Mankiller, "Hunter's Point was like a 'no man's land' that was constantly under siege."

Wilma did not find the adjustment easy. Her experiences in Riverbank had made her more confident, but she had no idea what kind of future she could hope for, and she often felt angry and alone. It was during this period that she began to turn to the San Francisco Indian Center for solidarity. "Everything seemed brighter at the Indian Center," she remembered later. "It became an oasis where I could share my feelings and frustrations with kids from similar backgrounds."

The center played an important role in a family crisis that occurred in 1960, when Wilma Mankiller was 15. That year, her 20-year-old brother, Robert, was killed in an accident in Washington State, where he had found a job picking apples. This sudden, violent loss left the Mankiller family stunned and dismayed, and they turned to the Indian Center for solace. Just being with other Indians, people who shared their values and understood their struggles, helped them cope with their grief.

As time passed, Wilma started to develop close friendships through her activities at the Indian Center. She played games, attended dance parties, listened to music—mostly rock and roll and soul—and had steady boyfriends. Meanwhile, she remained indifferent to school. "My

grades ranged from A to F, depending on the subject and my level of interest," she recalled. "Science and math were my downfalls, but I had an affinity for English and literature courses. . . . I was not much of a joiner. I did not go in for glee club or the yearbook staff or sports." More than anything, Wilma looked forward to the day when her high school years would be over.

When that day came, in June 1963, Mankiller quickly found a clerical job with a finance company and moved

Lights twinkle along the San Francisco–Oakland Bay Bridge as night falls over San Francisco. During their courtship in the summer of 1963, Mankiller and her future husband, Hugo Olaya, spent their evenings at restaurants, dance clubs, and other night spots all over the city.

in with her sister Frances. She was eager to get out into the world and to see how she would make it on her own. As it turned out, she would not be on her own for long. That summer, at a Latino dance in the city, she met her future husband, Hector Hugo Olaya de Bardi.

Hugo Olaya, as he was generally called, studied business and accounting at San Francisco State University. His family was quite wealthy, and he had been raised in a refined, aristocratic household. Wilma Mankiller found him charming and sophisticated. "I was a teenager, dating an exotic South American who was going to college and driving his own car," she remembered. "He was dashing and different and good-looking."

The two of them spent most of the summer together. Olaya took Mankiller to restaurants, nightclubs, and other places she had never been before. As the weeks went by, Olaya began to press her for a deeper commitment, and finally he told her he wanted to marry her. One October night, she accepted. "I thought that perhaps if I married Hugo," she recalled in her autobiography, "all my problems would disappear."

Mankiller's parents were not very happy with her plan, but they did not try to stop her. She and Olaya flew to Reno, Nevada, and on November 13, 1963, a few days before her 18th birthday, they married. After a brief honeymoon in Chicago, they found an apartment in San Francisco's Mission District and set up house. A few months later, Mankiller learned that she was pregnant, and in August 1964, she gave birth to a healthy daughter, whom they named Felicia.

Soon after Felicia was born, the family moved away from the Mission District and into a house in a quiet San Francisco neighborhood. Hugo continued his studies and took an evening job with Pan American Airlines; Wilma stayed home with her daughter, shopped, cooked, and cleaned. Less than two years later, her second daughter,

Gina, was born. Wilma was not yet 21. She had two children, a pleasant home, and security, but she was beginning to feel that she wanted more.

For the next few years, as she watched the many changes that were taking place around her, Mankiller's restlessness continued to grow. From time to time she would visit Haight-Ashbury, a neighborhood not far from her home where students, artists, and activists gathered to share their ideas. Passing in and out of crowded cafés, visiting shops selling incense, psychedelic posters, and health food, Mankiller hovered on the outskirts of this new generation looking for freedom and change. Later she wrote of her excursions to the area: "My daughters wore their shiny patent-leather shoes and little-girl dresses, and I looked like what I was at the time, a young housewife, who liked to observe what was going on around me, but was unwilling to get fully involved."

Hoping to change her life, but not sure how to go about it, in the late 1960s, Mankiller started taking courses at Skyline Junior College. She had no particular plan but took whatever subjects interested her, and for the first time ever, she found that she really enjoyed school. In time, she transferred to San Francisco State University. Later she wrote of her early college experience:

> One of the first things I did was to make sure I had all the resources necessary to "go the distance." I went directly to the library and found someone to show me how to use the material correctly. Then I read all I could find about taking proper notes and conducting research.

As Mankiller's world expanded beyond family concerns, Olaya began to worry. Above all, he wanted his home life to stay secure. He wanted to continue to play the role of the family provider, and he wanted his wife to stay at home. But Mankiller had no desire to stop what she had started. "I wanted to set my own limits and control my destiny," she wrote later. "I began to have dreams about more freedom and independence, and I finally came to understand that I did not have to live a life based on someone else's dreams."

4
AWAKENING

With the Indian occupation of Alcatraz, Wilma Mankiller's efforts to expand her world acquired a sharp focus. From the first few days of the takeover, she realized there was something she believed in passionately, and as the protest continued, her commitment to the Indian rights movement kept growing. More and more, Mankiller's Native American heritage became for her a source of deep pride, and as she grew increasingly conscious of her Indian identity, her ties with her siblings and parents, always strong, became even stronger. Several members of her family became as active in the movement as she was; her father understood that they were fighting for their people, and he was proud of them.

By 1969, Charley and Irene Mankiller had moved to a comfortable home to the south of the city, near Monterey. Most of their children were grown and out on their own, and Wilma Mankiller was happy to see her parents relaxing and enjoying themselves at last. Not long after she became involved in the action at Alcatraz, however, she learned that her father was gravely ill. He had developed a kidney disease that at the time was

Children celebrate Christmas at the American Indian Child Resource Center, an organization founded by Wilma Mankiller in 1974.

difficult to treat, and his doctor said he had little chance of surviving.

Wilma Mankiller had barely adjusted to this news when she became ill herself. Her first pregnancy had been accompanied by a kidney infection, and its symptoms now returned. After extensive testing, she was diagnosed with polycystic kidney disease—the same illness that was affecting her father. Fortunately, Mankiller was still very young, and in her case the disease had not progressed very far, but doctors predicted that by her mid-thirties she would suffer from kidney failure. Until then, there was little she could do but rest and be careful with her diet.

In the meantime, Mankiller did as much as she could for her father, who was steadily declining. All her life, she had looked to him for guidance and support, and seeing him struggle with his illness was very painful. "We had always shared an interest in political debate, in the community around us, and in books," she later commented. "Now we shared this family disease. It was so difficult to watch my father slowly leave us."

In February 1971, with his family gathered around his bed, Charley Mankiller died. His wife and children arranged to have him buried in Oklahoma, and the whole family traveled to their old homeland for the funeral. Mankiller described it later:

> It was a cold February day. We formed a line of cars and pickups and followed the hearse from the funeral home in Stilwell out to the graveyard. . . . As our procession of vehicles wound slowly down the road to the cemetery people came outside and stood in their yards to watch us pass. You could almost hear them saying, "There goes Charley Mankiller. They are bringing Charley Mankiller home."

Wilma Mankiller returned to California shortly after the funeral. Her work in the Indian community gave her some comfort, but she missed her father terribly. "We were all numb," she remembered. "The anchor that had always kept our family together was gone. In many ways, none of us would ever be the same again."

Meanwhile, between her studies at the university and her support of the Alcatraz takeover, Mankiller had been establishing her independence. By the time her Indian friends left Alcatraz in May 1971, she knew she could never go back to life as a housewife. Her husband disapproved of her activism, but she had developed the strength to oppose him. Olaya did not want his wife to travel without him, and when she told him she needed her own car, he refused her; Mankiller bought one anyway. Eventually she would see this act of defiance as her first real step toward freedom:

> Buying that little red car without my husband's consent or knowledge was my first act of rebellion against a lifestyle that I had come to believe was too narrow and confining for me. I wanted to break free to experience all the changes going on around me—the politics, literature, art, music, and the role of woman. But until I bought that little red Mazda, I was unwilling to take any risks to achieve more independence.

Free to travel where she pleased, Mankiller took her daughters to Native American events in many parts of California, Oregon, and Washington. One of her favorite places to visit was the home of the Pit River tribe in northern California. At the time, the tribe was involved in a fierce legal battle, and Mankiller decided to join their cause.

The dispute dated back to 1853, when the Pit River Indians were forced off their land and placed on a reservation so that white prospectors could mine gold in the region. Almost 100 years later, the federal government admitted that more than 3 million acres of land had been

Directors of the Intertribal Friendship House, an Indian community center in Oakland, attend a meeting in 1970. Mankiller worked with Native American organizations such as the Friendship House throughout the early 1970s.

taken from the tribe illegally. But instead of giving back the land, the government offered to pay the tribe a minimal fee of 47 cents an acre. The tribe rejected the offer.

The Pit River case, which had been in the courts for many years, spotlighted a prime example of the many Indian treaties that had yet to be honored by the U.S. government. For five years, Wilma Mankiller worked with the Pit River Indians to raise money for legal fees, and she helped the tribe prepare a letter to the U.S. president outlining their demands. Through her work with this community, she became familiar with the language of treaties and international law; starting from the ground up, she gained an education that would serve her well in later years.

Throughout the early 1970s, Mankiller also worked on a number of projects in the Bay Area Indian community. The demonstration at Alcatraz and the many other protests that it helped inspire had been very effective in drawing attention to the rights and needs of Native Americans. In the years that followed the enactment of

Nixon's self-determination policy, the BIA made more money available to the Indian community for improvements in housing, health, and education. For the first time, it allowed Indians across the country to develop and run such social programs themselves. There was much to be done, and Wilma Mankiller was eager to be a part of it.

One of Mankiller's earliest projects was to help set up the Native American Youth Center in East Oakland. As director of this organization, she hoped to create a place where young Indians could meet with friends, find help with problems at school or at work, and learn about their own heritage and history. Although, as she put it later, "she had no idea what she was doing," in almost no time, she had found a building, drafted volunteers to help paint it, put together some educational programs, and opened up the center. As the project got under way, she found a large number of Indians in the neighborhood who were enthusiastic and willing to help. Later she wrote of her gratitude for this support:

> When I had no clue where I was going to come up with the money for a renovation project, I went to a bar around the block . . . and asked for volunteers. Suddenly, to my great surprise and delight, I had several people on their feet, all ready to get to work. . . . It was in Oakland where I formed a belief that poor people, particularly poor American Indian people, have a lot more potential and many more answers to problems than they are ever given a chance to realize.

Hugo Olaya did not share Mankiller's commitment to improving the lives of others, and he continued to view her volunteer projects with distrust. Basically, her activism kept her from playing the role Olaya imagined a wife should play. Mankiller, too, was unhappy in the marriage—and had been for a long time. The two finally separated in 1974 and divorced about a year later.

After the separation, Mankiller and her daughters moved to Oakland, where the cost of living was lower. While continuing her studies at the university, Wilma took a job as a social worker at the Urban Indian Resource Center and was assigned to a number of projects designed to help Native American children. With a colleague, a Blackfoot Indian named Betty Cooper, she conducted a study of child abuse and neglect in the Native American community. Cooper and Mankiller learned that among Native Americans, child abuse and neglect were usually

In 1974, Mankiller moved with her daughters to Oakland, an industrial city on the eastern shore of San Francisco Bay.

connected with alcohol and drug abuse, and they advised social agencies to concentrate on treating these problems. Mankiller also worked on a project involving the foster-care placement and adoption of Indian children. Discovering that 25 percent of Indian children were being placed in homes outside of their culture, Mankiller and others in the organization worked with a group of attorneys to develop the Indian Child Welfare Act, which made it illegal for Indian children to be taken from their tribal culture.

According to Cooper, Mankiller approached her work with skill and enthusiasm. The Native American community was growing more confident at that time, and those who worked at the center were able to accomplish a great deal. Cooper later said of this period:

> Everything was happening. There was so much change in Oakland, in Indian people. You could just see their strength surfacing. And Wilma was right there. It was always a pleasure to associate with her, to share her ideas. Our convictions were the same. We both believed that changes had to be made at the heart of the community and that's how our people were going to be strong.

Through her work in the Bay Area Indian community, Wilma Mankiller developed skills that would contribute to her success in the years ahead. She learned to work with Indians from many different tribes, to interact well with government agencies, and to organize large projects. She also earned a reputation as an excellent grant-proposal writer. Betty Cooper later recalled, "Wilma was recognized for many things, but her writing skills were her greatest gift to the Indian community. She helped write proposals for many organizations that are still operating in the 1990s."

During this period of growth and optimism, many of the Indians who had moved to the city under the BIA's relocation program began to think about returning to

Trainees take a break at Oakland's Pacific Automotive Center, an Indian trade school, in 1972. After President Richard Nixon introduced his self-determination policy in 1971, government aid for this and other Indian-run programs increased dramatically.

their tribal lands. Cooper remembered: "It was almost as if a dream would come, or an inspiration would come, and people would say, 'It's time for me to go home, it's time for me to get out of the city.' They'd tell me this, and I'd tell them 'Don't deny it. Go home. Your people need you.'" For Wilma Mankiller, too, the peaceful hills of Oklahoma began to seem like the perfect place to make a new start. There, she thought, in the country of her childhood, her daughters would grow up closer to nature and their Cherokee heritage. Feeling she needed a place where she could relax and live more quietly than she had in the recent past, Mankiller thought that a home in the country might be better for her as well. In 1976, shortly after her mother decided to make the same move, she followed her instincts and returned to Mankiller Flats.

5

BEING OF GOOD MIND

In the summer of 1976, Mankiller said good-bye to her Oakland friends and co-workers, packed everything she owned into a rented truck, gathered her daughters and the family dog, and set off. A few days later, she arrived at Mankiller Flats, where her mother welcomed her.

In the coming weeks, Wilma Mankiller built a small wooden house on her family's land down the road from her mother's home. Gradually, she settled in. For her daughters, who had always lived in the city, Oklahoma was a little bewildering at first, but there were so many things to do that they adjusted quickly. The nearest neighbors were miles away, but there were animals to play with and acres of woods to explore. Most of Mankiller's brothers and sisters gradually moved east as well, and soon she and her daughters had a large number of supportive family members close at hand. Later she wrote:

> I recall the day I was really and truly home. It was some time after our return. I went into Stilwell to take care of some business. I was walking across the lawn of the Adair County Courthouse, and I spied some old Cherokee men sitting on the benches. They were chewing tobacco and talking over the world's most important problems, just as old Cherokee men have done in Stilwell for a long, long time. As I walked by them, I heard one of them say to the others, "There goes John Mankiller's granddaughter." Those five simple words were sweet to hear.

Oklahoma Cherokees attend an annual folklore festival in Eureka Springs, Arkansas, in the mid-1970s, around the time Mankiller returned to her childhood home. As government funding for Native Americans increased across the country, traditional arts such as pottery, basket-making, music, and dance enjoyed a revival in the Cherokee Nation.

In some ways, Cherokee territory had remained very much like the country Mankiller remembered from her childhood, but there were also aspects of Cherokee life that had greatly changed. In the 1960s, President Lyndon B. Johnson's vow to "end poverty in America" had brought more federal assistance to Cherokee families. Meanwhile, the Indian activism of the late 1960s, although focused on the empowerment of urban Indians, had affected rural Indian communities as well. Urban activists had inspired the Cherokees to draw strength from their cultural heritage and stand up for the right to control their own lives.

For the Cherokees, the enactment of Nixon's self-determination policy in 1971 carried special meaning, as it restored to them a power that had long been withheld. After their territory was divided into allotments in 1906, the Cherokees had been deprived of the right to control their own government. Congress had granted the U.S. president the power to appoint a principal chief for the tribe, and this chief was to appoint the other tribal officers, leaving the rest of the Cherokee people out of the selection process. In 1971, this ruling changed, and for the first time in 64 years, the Cherokees were able to elect their own principal chief. Four years later, they regained the right to elect the rest of their tribal officers, so that once again the tribal government was a true democracy, answerable to the Cherokee people.

When Wilma Mankiller returned to Oklahoma in 1976, the Cherokee Nation was rebuilding itself, just as it had twice before in the tribe's history. Ross Swimmer had been elected principal chief. Swimmer was determined to improve the economy in the 14 counties under the Cherokee Nation's jurisdiction so that more people could find jobs. Under his leadership, the tribe bought more land, started new industries, brought new businesses into the area, and opened a job-training center.

The Spring River passes a wooded promontory in northeastern Oklahoma. Surrounded by woods, streams, and wide-open spaces, Mankiller and her children found their Oklahoma home very different from the urban world they had left behind.

The standard of living among the Cherokees had clearly improved, but Mankiller could see that many people in the area were still demoralized and living in terrible poverty. Although she had not intended to continue her activism in Oklahoma, what she saw made her angry, and she believed strongly that she could do something to change it. In the fall of 1976, when the time came for her to find work, she knew exactly where to look, and before long she had landed a job at the Cherokee Nation complex in Tahlequah.

Ross Swimmer, a banker from Oklahoma City, became principal chief of the Cherokee Nation in 1975.

In her new position as economic-stimulus coordinator, it was Mankiller's task to encourage Cherokees to get university training in environmental sciences and health and then return to their communities, bringing their new skills and higher earning power with them. Mankiller threw herself into the job with the same energy and spirit she had shown in California. She knew she would soon be able to put her grant-writing skills to good use, but first she wanted to become familiar with the rural communities where people needed the most help. Going from one small Cherokee village to the next, she held meetings and listened carefully to the people as they talked about what they would like to do to make their lives better. Enlightened by this experience, Mankiller found herself "full of ideas about programs and services," and in early 1979, she was made a program-development specialist. Although she was already very busy, she decided to complete the coursework required for her bachelor's degree in social sciences, and eventually she began taking graduate classes in community planning at the University of Arkansas. Then, one fall day, her life changed abruptly.

On November 8, 1979, Mankiller was driving home from the university, looking forward to relaxing after a busy week. She had spent the previous evening at home with two of her cousins. Sitting in front of the wood-burning stove, they had talked about Cherokee medicine and its uses; they knew that Cherokee medicine people could use their powers to cause harm as well as to heal. They had been sitting and talking for some time when they began to notice something unusual happening outside the house. They could hear something calling from the woods, and as they looked out of the windows, they saw vague shapes moving in the trees and in the sky. As their eyes adjusted to the darkness, they realized that a flock of owls had gathered around the house. The incident made Mankiller uneasy. Remembering it later, she wrote:

> Some Cherokees, including my own family, are taught to beware of owls. We were told that a *dedonsek,* "one who makes bad medicine," could change into an owl and travel through the night skies to visit Cherokee homes. That usually brought bad luck. I had heard stories that if owls came close to the house, it often meant bad news was coming.

The next day, as Mankiller was traveling down the highway, a car moving in the opposite direction suddenly pulled out to pass another vehicle and collided with her car head-on. The driver of the car that struck her was one of her closest friends, Sherry Morris, who was killed instantly. Wilma Mankiller was so badly injured that paramedics at the scene of the accident at first thought she was dead.

Soon after returning to Oklahoma, Mankiller began taking graduate courses in community planning at the University of Arkansas in Fayetteville, about an hour's drive from her home.

Mankiller woke up in a hospital bed, barely able to move. Yet her feelings, she recalled later, went far beyond suffering:

> One leg was crushed, one broken. My ribs were broken. My nose and other facial bones were too. All I remember now is how I felt. I was dying, yet it was a beautiful and spiritual experience, warm and loving, soft. I no longer feared death. I saw how precious health and life are, how important it is to do something good with your life and to share. I realized how insignificant you are in the totality of things. It's a precious thing to be here and take part in the world.

It took several months for Mankiller to recover from the accident. For the first three weeks, no one told her who the driver of the other car had been. Finally Morris's husband broke the news. Mankiller was devastated. Her grief, coupled with her own physical pain, bore down heavily on her spirit as she waited for her bones to heal.

While she was in the hospital, Mankiller received visits from tribal elders, who offered her traditional Cherokee medicine and helped remind her of the ancient philosophy of life that she called "being of good mind." She remembered:

> The medicine men and the elders talked to me about how we should be as a people. They showed me the sacred wampum belts that teach the truth of Cherokee life: that we should have good minds, consider everything in the world—including nature—as brothers and sisters. We should not be judgmental, but accept all as family and focus on the positive, no matter what circumstances you find yourself in.

As the weeks went by, plastic surgery repaired the damage to Mankiller's face, and most of her other injuries gradually healed. The bones in her right leg, however, had been completely shattered, and her doctors told her at one point that she might not walk again. To Mankiller's relief, after 17 operations, her leg was fully repaired, and she was sent home from the hospital with a pair of crutches.

But her ordeal was not over. During the following weeks, she gradually began to lose control of her muscles. Remembering her confusion, she later wrote:

> Just when I thought I was finally getting well, my muscles began to weaken. I couldn't hold my toothbrush or my hairbrush, and I couldn't control my speech or my facial muscles. It was very frightening. At first I thought it was from the accident. I kept going to the doctor and saying "something's wrong with me." Then one day I was watching a muscular dystrophy telethon on TV. A woman was describing the symptoms and I thought, "That's what I have."

Mankiller called a muscular dystrophy center, which referred her to a specialist. A short time later, the doctor diagnosed myasthenia gravis, a rare nervous-system disorder related to muscular dystrophy. The condition was quickly getting worse. "I was totally dysfunctional," Mankiller recalls. "My head wouldn't hold up. My eyes didn't work right."

In November 1980, Mankiller returned to the hospital for another round of surgery. After an operation in which doctors repaired muscle and nerve damage in her chest, she underwent an intensive program of chemotherapy, a process commonly used to treat cancer patients. Looking back on the experience in 1988, she told an interviewer:

> After the surgery I was on a life support system. Finally I got angry. I said, "Get me out of here and off this stuff. I'm not going to take this any more. I'm going to participate in getting well." The doctors thought I'd have to stay on the support system for three weeks. Instead I came off it in three days. Once I took charge of my life, my body gradually began to heal.

Mankiller would receive chemotherapy for several years. Although she endured some troublesome side effects, including significant weight gain, in the end, the treatment was successful.

After more than a year of struggling to regain her health, Mankiller was eager to get on with her life, and in December 1980, she returned to work. Although it did not take long for her to settle back in, she could tell that in many ways she was now a different person. Later she would compare her two selves—the woman before and the woman after the accident—and reflect on what had changed:

> Before the accident I had a hard edge. I spent a lot of time being angry at injustices against people in general and the Cherokee in particular.... Coming so close to death moved me beyond the ego to the calm. I can't imagine what could rattle me now. I also became a lot tougher and firmer, without becoming mean-spirited. I don't worry so much about little things. I focus more on the good.

Back at work, Mankiller threw herself into her job with the same energy and enthusiasm as ever. She wanted to see the lives of her people improve, and she had concrete ideas about how she could help them. Her experience with the Cherokee Nation thus far had reinforced her belief that communities were the most important basic structure in Cherokee society. Because the Cherokees in Oklahoma lived in small towns and villages rather than on a reservation, Mankiller sensed that it was through these communities, more than through the tribal government, that the tribe formed its identity. "In the old days when you would identify yourself Cherokee to Cherokee, you would give your name and your clan," she once pointed out. "Today people identify themselves by their community." Mankiller came to believe that community development—improving living conditions and social services such as health care and education—was an important first step toward economic development—creating jobs and income.

Presenting the government with a grant proposal that explained her philosophy, Mankiller secured hundreds of thousands of dollars in federal funding. Her first large-scale project was carried out in Bell, a particularly poor backwoods community about 10 miles from Mankiller Flats. Bell was so isolated that many of its families had no electricity or running water. When Mankiller first approached the community, the people there were frustrated and angry. Their unemployment rate was 60 percent, their children were dropping out of school, and their lives were disrupted by fighting and drinking.

Mankiller hoped that her project would not only help the citizens of Bell rebuild their homes but also "restore their faith in themselves." To achieve these goals, she designed the program in such a way that people would be involved in solving their own problems. When the project was completed, Mankiller explained her approach:

Workers paint a house in Bell, the Oklahoma community where Mankiller helped residents set up a water and housing project.

If you look to the people in a community themselves and ask them where they want to go and what they want to do, they know. Sometimes all they need is some outside help to figure out how to get there. We struck a bargain with them, a sort of partnership. What we told them was "We'll raise the money for you, we'll organize, we'll act as facilitators, we'll give you times and places you need to do things, if you will commit to build these houses, build a new water system, rehabilitate the community building . . . so that we're not doing it for you."

At first it sounded strange to people, but as they thought about it and talked about it, they saw it was about the only way they were going to get what they wanted—water and housing. Every single Indian family in that community showed up and put in time on the water system. Each family had to contribute two months of labor in order to participate in the project. That was the bargain. They laid a 16-mile pipeline; they rehabilitated 20 houses and they built some new houses. But something else happened that is more important. For the first time that community came together and did something as a group. They began to see that they had the power and ability to change their community.

The project in Bell was a big success. It received national attention and eventually became a model for other Indian tribes who were trying to improve their conditions. In the months following the project's completion, Mankiller continued to raise funds for Cherokee communities, always stressing self-help as a source of self-esteem. A year later, fully recovered from her accident and illness, she founded the Community Development Department of the Cherokee Nation and became its first director.

6
BUILDING UNITY AND INDEPENDENCE

From 1980 to 1983, Ross Swimmer, principal chief of the Cherokee Nation, watched Wilma Mankiller do more for Cherokee communities than he had ever dreamed possible in such a short time. Not only did Mankiller seem to understand what had to be accomplished in each community, but she was able to turn her ideas into action. In the three years Swimmer had known her, Mankiller had raised millions of dollars in grant money, organized enormous projects, and motivated hundreds of people. Ross Swimmer knew that Mankiller had the ability to get things done, and in 1983, when he decided to run for a third four-year term as principal chief, he asked her to run with him for the position of deputy chief.

Mankiller was flattered by the request; she was also somewhat surprised. For one thing, she knew that she and Chief Swimmer had different political philosophies. Swimmer came from an urban background and categorized himself as a conservative Republican. During his first two terms as principal chief, he had worked on making the Cherokee Nation less dependent on government "handouts." To improve the tribe's finances, he had opened a number of tribal businesses, including a motel,

Wilma Mankiller, pictured in the early 1980s, impressed Principal Chief Ross Swimmer with her achievements in community service. Swimmer asked her to be his running mate in the 1983 Cherokee Nation elections.

a restaurant, an electronics firm, and a cattle and poultry ranch. Most of these enterprises were quite successful.

Mankiller, on the other hand, was deeply involved in helping poor, rural communities in the Cherokee Nation. She considered herself a liberal Democrat, believing it was the government's responsibility to provide such basic necessities as housing and health care wherever they were needed.

Still, she and Swimmer agreed on a major point: it was important to help the Cherokees become more self-sufficient. In Mankiller's opinion, helping members of the tribe work toward independence was an important part of helping them build a strong cultural identity. This shared goal, along with their respect for each other, had always helped Mankiller and Chief Swimmer work well together.

Mankiller had never planned to run for tribal office; nor was she eager to leave the community development department. She found her work there exciting and challenging. In fact, she could think of nothing more rewarding than helping people in poor, isolated Cherokee communities solve their problems. If she were to become deputy chief, she would only be indirectly involved in community development. Yet she also knew that as deputy chief she would be able to learn and grow in ways she had never considered before; she would be contributing to all aspects of the Cherokee Nation. After thinking the matter over, she decided that the opportunity was too good to pass up. She agreed to be Ross Swimmer's running mate.

Mankiller was completely unprepared for what happened next: her candidacy created an uproar. Older members of the tribe refused to support her—not because they considered her unqualified for the position, but because she was a woman. "It was the first time that I

Ross Swimmer and Wilma Mankiller pause during their 1983 campaign. Although the political views of the two candidates differed sharply, their shared commitment to Cherokee independence made them a strong team.

felt disliked simply because I am a woman," she said later. "It was really a tough time."

To Mankiller, the prejudice she encountered as she ran for office was a clear demonstration of the way in which the tribe's original culture and belief system had changed. Before the Cherokees' exposure to European culture,

Cherokee women had played a prominent role in the tribe, both in their own families and in tribal councils. Because women created life by giving birth to the tribe's children, they were generally treated with honor and respect. Cherokee society was based on a matrilineal family system; that is, individuals traced their ancestors through their mother's family line instead of through their father's. Cherokee children were considered part of their mother's clan and were given their mother's family name, not their father's. In fact, although children knew their fathers, they were not even considered related to them by blood. When a Cherokee man married, he was expected to build a house for his wife—which was then considered her property—or else go to his mother-in-law's house to live with his new wife. If a couple divorced, the husband moved out. The shift to a male-oriented or patrilineal system—and the sexism that came with it—occurred as Cherokees adopted non-Indian ways.

In traditional Cherokee culture, according to Mankiller, women also played important political roles. She explained:

> Women were the center of the family and the tribe. They trained the chiefs and had their own council. The head of their council had a powerful voice in government. And women sometimes went to war alongside their husbands and sons.
>
> In the early 1800s, for the sake of survival, the tribe adopted a system similar to the federal government's, which had no place for women. But the people continued to pass on the tradition of nurturing and assertiveness to both genders. That's why it never occurred to me that anyone would be concerned about having a female as Deputy Chief.

As the election campaign got under way, Swimmer's opponent tried hard to capitalize on the doubts and fears of prejudiced Cherokee voters. Even some of Swimmer's advisers worried that if Mankiller became deputy chief it would create difficulties for the Cherokee Nation. Some claimed that her election would create controversy and distract the tribe from more important matters. They urged Swimmer to change his mind, but the chief held firm. "I was told the last thing our ticket needed was a female," he later said. "But I couldn't buy that. Wilma was the absolute best person for the job."

Encouraged by Swimmer's confidence, Mankiller responded to the criticism leveled against her by concentrating on her ideas for rebuilding the tribe. When voters raised the issue of her gender, she talked instead of her work in community development or her commitment to improving health care by expanding overcrowded hospitals in rural areas. The Swimmer/Mankiller campaign posters promised that together the two leaders would "make things happen." Little by little, the strategy took effect. A small minority continued to attack Mankiller; one person even said that if she were elected it would be "an affront to God." But by election day, most of the Cherokee people had decided to give her a chance. Swimmer was reelected principal chief, and Wilma Mankiller became the first female deputy chief in the history of the Cherokee Nation.

Mankiller had hoped that, once elected, she would be treated no differently than her predecessors. She soon discovered that things were not going to be that simple. One of her duties was to serve as president of the Tribal Council, which at that time consisted primarily of older men. At her first council session, according to Mankiller, "One man kept interrupting me as I tried to conduct the meeting. He kept citing obsolete rules or things that he had made up. He was a former boxer, a real macho guy." Instead of getting upset, Mankiller allowed the man to think he had gotten the best of her. But at the next meeting, she made sure she had control of all the

This 1880 photograph shows a young Cherokee woman who, like many other "mixed-bloods," has adopted non-Indian dress.

microphones. "When someone started getting out of line I just turned off their microphone," she said. "Then we were able to get down to business."

As Wilma Mankiller's colleagues and constituents came to know her, much of the public excitement over the issue of her gender died down. In more subtle ways, however, sexist attitudes continued to affect her throughout her term as deputy chief. "I was very conscious of the fact that I was the first female Deputy Chief and people were watching me," she said later. "I wanted to make sure I did a good job. I didn't want to miss any meetings or anything and have it blamed on my being a woman."

Pushing herself harder than ever, Mankiller took on one Cherokee problem after another. One of her first causes as deputy chief concerned the troubled relations between full-blood and mixed-blood Cherokees. It was a problem that dated back to the early 1800s, and one she had been aware of all her life.

When Wilma Mankiller was a child, she had learned from her older relatives that much earlier, when the original land of the Cherokees was being overrun by settlers, the tribe had decided that their best chance of survival lay in adopting non-Indian ways. Some Cherokees married non-Indians, and the children from these marriages became the first mixed-bloods. The name was used to distinguish them from full-bloods, who had Cherokee ancestry on both sides of their family tree.

From the beginning, the terms *mixed-blood* and *full-blood* had connotations that went beyond their literal meaning. Not only did mixed-bloods have non-Indians in their family background, but they tended to live in the style of non-Indians as well. Many adopted the ways of the settlers, shifting the focus of their lives away from the community and toward the acquisition of personal wealth. The full-bloods, on the other hand, felt threatened by the idea of adopting non-Indian culture. Although they took on some of the new ways, they made a conscious effort to maintain their communities and their Cherokee culture, religion, and language. They usually appeared less affluent than mixed-bloods because they accumulated fewer possessions.

When the Cherokees were asked to leave their homeland and move west to Indian Territory, those who moved willingly—regardless of their family background—were referred to as mixed-bloods. The Cherokees who resisted became known as full-bloods—even though their ancestors were not necessarily all Cherokees. The differences between the two groups were subtle and complex, and for the next 150 years, mixed-bloods and full-bloods frequently took opposite positions on tribal issues, much as the Republican and Democratic parties do in Washington today.

By the mid-1980s, almost all the Cherokees in Oklahoma had some non-Indian blood, but the political division remained. Generally, the mixed-bloods believed that the Cherokee Nation should pursue a course of progress and economic growth, while the full-bloods maintained that modernization would destroy the identity of the tribe. The two sides argued over many issues, such as whether the tribe should spend money on a program to teach the Cherokee language or whether a non-Indian should be appointed to head a Cherokee company if he or she had better qualifications than Cherokee applicants.

Because she identified with both of them, Wilma Mankiller hoped that she could bring these two factions of the tribe together. Her father had been a full-blood, and she had been raised in a fairly traditional Cherokee household until her family relocated to San Francisco. After the move, she had been educated at non-Indian schools and assimilated into an urban environment. Having experienced both ways of life, Mankiller remained a strong advocate of Cherokee tradition, but she also believed that too much isolation would keep the tribe from fulfilling its potential in the modern world. In her own life, she tried to blend the mixed-blood and full-blood viewpoints into a philosophy that balanced modern and traditional ways. She believed that a balanced approach was best for the tribe as well. Mankiller once explained:

> In my father's generation there was a sense of having only two options. One is that you didn't interact with the larger society at all and remained a traditional Cherokee. In fact one of my uncles thought you were totally lost if you went to school past the eighth grade because you became acculturated. The other option was that in order to make it in the world you had to give your heritage up completely. There was no middle point.
>
> In my generation, we're trying to figure out a balance between the two worlds. There are extremes on both sides. There are those who have turned their backs on being Cherokee. Then we have a few who refuse to speak much English and think children should only play stickball, not baseball or football. They are suspicious of the non-Indian world, and think too much assimilation will cause one to stop thinking Cherokee. I think the most positive thing happening is that people are beginning to understand that they can live and work in a very modern, fast-moving society, but also celebrate who they are as Cherokees and maintain a sense of self.

Mankiller initiated a number of projects to help the Cherokee tribe maintain its unique culture. She secured money to expand the Cherokee Heritage Center, a museum that houses a replica of a 17th-century Cherokee village. She also helped develop the Institute for Cherokee Literacy, an organization that teaches students to read and write the Cherokee language.

Mankiller was able to give Cherokee full-bloods more voice in the tribal council by persuading the tribe to change the way council members got elected. Previously, all members of the council had been elected at large by the entire tribe. But that meant that the people chosen usually came from the most populated region under Cherokee jurisdiction, the area within 50 miles of the

Cherokee Nation. Under Mankiller's new system, Cherokee territory was divided into districts based on population, and each district was able to elect its own representative. That way, even the most isolated communities always had someone on the tribal council to speak for them, and full-bloods—most of whom lived in rural areas—had a better chance of getting elected.

Once they had better representation, the more traditional full-bloods began to understand that interaction

A young Cherokee girl helps recreate history at Tsa-la-gi, a reconstructed 17th-century Indian village at the Cherokee Heritage Center in Tahlequah. As deputy chief, Mankiller helped increase the funding for this and other cultural organizations.

with the modern world could strengthen the Cherokee Nation instead of weakening it. At the same time, the success of different cultural programs helped the more assimilated mixed-bloods understand that maintaining Cherokee values and cultural identity was vital to the tribe's long-term survival. With Mankiller's encouragement, the tribe was able to work toward greater unity.

By the time Wilma Mankiller had been deputy chief for two years, any doubts she had about the job had vanished. She was involved in everything, and she loved every minute of it. Then, one day in 1985, Ross Swimmer called her into his office and invited her to sit down. Looking her straight in the eyes, he told her some very surprising news. President Ronald Reagan had asked him to become the director of the Bureau of Indian Affairs.

"I was stunned," Mankiller remembered later. "If Ross took the job in Washington, it meant I was Principal Chief. I didn't want it. It would change my whole life." Mankiller left Swimmer's office in a daze. She needed time to think—to decide whether she was ready to take on the responsibility Swimmer was offering her. A few hours later, she returned and gave the principal chief her answer: she would do it. For the first time ever, a woman was about to become principal chief of the Cherokee Nation.

7

THE CAMPAIGN

In December 1985, at an inaugural ceremony at the Cherokee Nation headquarters, Wilma Mankiller stepped up to the podium wearing a dark blue suit, a white blouse, and a simple necklace of pearls. To the audience, the soft-spoken, unpretentious 40-year-old woman may not have looked like an Indian leader. But as Mankiller repeated the oath of office for principal chief, the conviction in her voice told all who had come to listen that she was committed to the tribe and its future.

Principal Chief Mankiller gave a short speech when the ceremony was over, reassuring the audience that she planned to "stay on the same path" as her predecessor. She wanted to allay some concerns that had developed over Ross Swimmer's departure—and the woman who was stepping into his position.

In the months following her inauguration, Mankiller carried out her promise by continuing to look for new sources of income for the tribe. She also tried to implement some of the ideas she had developed separately from Swimmer, including new health care and housing programs. Mankiller was frustrated to find her initiatives blocked by tribal council members who were still loyal to former chief Swimmer and reluctant to spend money on social services.

Wilma Mankiller, the first woman ever to serve as principal chief of the Cherokee Nation, delivers a speech near the beginning of her administration.

For her entire political career, Mankiller had prided herself on her ability to get things done. Now, as principal chief, she should have been in a position to do even more. Yet without the support and confidence of the rest of the Cherokee government, she found that her options were limited. "It was as though I had all the responsibility with none of the authority," she recalled. "So I just coped."

During her first few months as principal chief, Mankiller's job brought her little satisfaction; her personal life, on the other hand, was blossoming. For many years, Wilma Mankiller had been close friends with Charlie Soap, a handsome Cherokee full-blood. When Mankiller first met him, Charlie Soap was working for the Indian Housing Authority, a government agency that operated in conjunction with the Cherokee Nation. Later, when they worked together on the Bell project, Mankiller and Soap discovered they had much in common. They were the same age, and both had spent their early years on Cherokee land in Oklahoma. They had both been married before, and both had children. Most important, Soap, like Mankiller, believed in maintaining Cherokee values and remained deeply committed to the Cherokee tribe. Mankiller later said of their relationship:

> We . . . did not pay much attention to each other on a personal level until after the Bell project was concluded. Instead, we first developed a fine working relationship, and that led to a solid and strong friendship. That proved to be the best foundation for us when we finally realized we were in love.

Early in 1986, Wilma Mankiller and Charlie Soap became engaged. The couple exchanged rings, but they decided to wait before announcing their plans to the public. They both worried about what the tribe would think if Mankiller married; some older tribe members, they suspected, might expect the new principal chief to

Mankiller attends a Tahlequah powwow with Charlie Soap, a longtime community leader acclaimed for his skill in Native American dance. The couple married in October 1986.

step down. By October 1986, Mankiller felt secure enough in her new position to hold the wedding, but she took special care to reassure the tribe that her marriage would not affect her duties as principal chief. She and Charlie Soap were married in a quiet ceremony. In keeping with Cherokee tradition, Soap moved into Mankiller's house on Mankiller Flats.

As Wilma Mankiller approached the end of her term as principal chief in 1987, she felt ambivalent about running for election to a second term. To sort out her feelings, she turned to her husband. She was tired of struggling with the tribal council over social issues. On the other hand, she knew that she could do a lot more for the tribe if she were elected in her own right. By obtaining the majority of votes, she would have much more influence on the tribal council than she had been able to exert when she succeeded Ross Swimmer to the position. Charlie Soap encouraged her to fight for a second term, but Mankiller was still hesitant.

Then people began arriving at the front door of the little house on Mankiller Flats, asking Wilma Mankiller not to run. Some objected to her progressive ideas, and others disapproved of her because she was a woman. Whatever their reasons, the fact that they would drive all the way down the dirt road to her home just to tell her to withdraw from the election made Mankiller furious. "If one more family comes by and tells me not to run, I'm running," she finally told her husband. A short while later there was a knock at the door. Wilma Mankiller began her election campaign for principal chief the next day.

"I was running against three strong, politically connected men," Mankiller remembered later. "But I liked the challenge." Her primary opponent, Perry Wheeler, was a funeral parlor director and a former deputy chief.

He had run for principal chief in 1983, but lost to Swimmer. Mankiller knew Wheeler was telling voters that too much change was a bad thing. He was trying to convince people that modernizing Cherokee communities and bringing in new businesses would result in a loss of tribal identity. If they elected Wilma Mankiller, Wheeler argued, the Cherokees would become completely assimilated into American society.

Mankiller knew that Wheeler was wrong, but she also knew there were plenty of Cherokees who would agree with him. Preparing herself for a long, tough campaign, she planned her strategy carefully. In order to win, Mankiller had to appeal to a broad range of people with different needs and beliefs. The key to success, as she saw it, was to convince the electorate that while her plans might not please everyone, they would benefit the tribe as a whole.

Unlike Wheeler, Mankiller believed that for the Cherokee Nation, change and interaction with the outside world was not only inevitable but important. In speeches to groups in towns and villages, she explained that cooperation with mainstream institutions such as the state of Oklahoma and the federal government in Washington did not mean the Cherokees would lose their identity. On the contrary, she argued, by negotiating from positions of strength and confidence, the Cherokee tribe could become a powerful regional presence, just as it had been in the late 19th century.

Other Indian tribes had tried to isolate themselves, Mankiller pointed out, and they had failed. By shutting the door on economic opportunity, those tribes had only become poorer, and consequently more dependent on the federal government. And as the Cherokees knew well from their own history, that was not a good position to be in.

Photographed in the 1930s, Cherokee women wear clothing that incorporates both European and Indian styles. As Mankiller explained during her campaign, the Cherokees had a long tradition of female leadership; it was only as the tribe adopted European ways that the Cherokee government began to exclude women.

As the campaign progressed, Mankiller outlined the many problems that faced the Cherokee tribe. In 1987, tribal membership was growing quickly; at the same time, federal budget cuts made under President Reagan were making it harder to provide services to those in need. The Cherokees would have to deal with a severe shortage of low-income housing. Health care and nutrition programs had been cut back because of funding losses. As many as 35 percent of Cherokee students dropped out of high school before graduating. And 15 percent of the Cherokee work force was unemployed. Although this rate was lower than in some Indian tribes, it was much higher than the unemployment rate in the United States as a whole.

Mankiller agreed that new business investment brought money and jobs into the tribe, but she also insisted that the most effective approach to economic development was to attack social problems head-on. If she was elected chief, she said, she would do everything in her power not only to promote new business but also to raise money for housing and community development, to expand existing health care programs, and to improve educational opportunities for adults as well as children. "I'd like to see whole, healthy communities again," she told her audiences during the campaign. "Communities in which tribe members would have access to adequate health care, higher education if they want it, a decent place to live and a decent place to work, and a strong commitment to tribal language and culture."

Just as she had done in her earlier community-development work with the Cherokee Nation, Wilma Mankiller spent much of her time talking with people in the communities she wanted to help. She spoke of her own experiences with poverty—as a child on Mankiller Flats and later in San Francisco. She recounted her struggle after her accident and subsequent illness to heal herself and approach the world with a "good mind." Mankiller told her audience:

> As a result of my experience, I came to the conclusion that everyday people have a lot more to contribute than they have the opportunity to materialize. I want to get you involved in articulating your own visions. I see a lot of beauty and intelligence and sharing in our communities. And I would like to build on that. But we have to stop believing in magic. No one's going to pull us out but ourselves.

Mankiller's speeches were heartfelt and inspiring, but her appeal was based on more than words. Through her direct contact with the Cherokee people, she was able to demonstrate that she was a fair-minded, caring, and knowledgeable person who believed in action. James Morrison, director of the Oaks Indian Center, a home for displaced children, discussed Mankiller's campaign in a 1992 interview:

> I went to listen to her talk, and I heard some questions being asked. So I talked to those people and found out what their concerns were, things like "what's going to happen with that new hospital?" and then I went back to them later to see how she'd responded. I was really interested to see what she would do. And you know, everyone that she told she would get back to, she did. A lot of people say, "well I'm gonna do this, and I'm gonna do that," and then you never hear from them again. But Wilma is very honest. She'd say "I'm gonna get some answers." Then she would come back and tell these people, "this is what's happening, and this is what we foresee will happen in the future." And that's the kind of person I like to deal with. It's either, "we can do it or we can't do it, or we can try, but I can't make you any promises." When you've got a person like that you always know where you stand.

Thanks to the donations Mankiller received from her supporters, she was able to get her message across. During the campaign, northeastern Oklahoma was blanketed with an unprecedented number of billboard, radio, and even television advertisements publicizing her philosophy

Wilma Mankiller and Charlie Soap mingle with guests at a Lodge of the Cherokees reception in Tahlequah near the end of the 1987 campaign. As the election approached, Soap became one of Mankiller's most persuasive spokesmen.

and urging people to "Vote for Wilma Mankiller!" Even more important, Mankiller once again made a point of visiting voters in every county in the Cherokee Nation.

When the election was only a few weeks away, Mankiller became very ill with a kidney infection and had to spend two weeks in the hospital. One of her opponents saw her illness as an opportunity to weaken her campaign and started a rumor. She later recalled, "When I was in the hospital before the election, there was a telephone campaign going on saying that I wasn't expected to live. I talked to a television reporter who said he had been called and told I had been taken to Houston on a life flight."

But nasty rumors were not the only problem Mankiller had to contend with. As election day drew closer, she learned that a number of older, more traditional Cherokees still objected to having a woman serve as principal chief. When she had been running for deputy chief, her advisers had warned her not to get drawn into a debate over gender and leadership. But this time, she and her husband Charlie Soap felt that sexist attitudes could not go unanswered. So, when Mankiller wanted to address certain tradition-minded men of the tribe, Charlie Soap became her spokesman.

A full-blood who was fluent in the Cherokee language, Soap knew that he could win the respect of traditional Cherokees. He was able to communicate Mankiller's ideas to his conservative tribesmen in their own language. He reminded them that a female principal chief was in keeping with Cherokee tradition as it had been before the influence of settlers altered it. For the remainder of the campaign, while Wilma Mankiller continued to propose solutions to pressing Cherokee problems, Charlie Soap worked to convince traditional Cherokees that Mankiller was the right person to lead their nation.

As election day drew near, it became clear that the Cherokee people felt strongly about this race and that voter turnout would be high. According to informal polls, Mankiller was the leading candidate, but her campaign staff warned her that it would be a close contest. On July 20, 1987, she waited at home with her husband while the votes were counted. Finally, late that evening, she received a call from the election officials. She had received 45 percent of the ballots; the runner-up, Perry Wheeler, had received only 29 percent.

According to tribal law, a candidate needed to win more than 50 percent of the votes in order to be elected, and a runoff election between Mankiller and Wheeler was held a few days later. This time Mankiller won decisively. Ten years after returning to her homeland in Oklahoma, Wilma Mankiller was elected principal chief of the Cherokee Nation, one of the most prominent Indian tribes in North America.

8

THE LIFE OF A PRINCIPAL CHIEF

After the election, Wilma Mankiller continued to work hard and live simply. Usually she would get up before the sun and begin her workday at home, in the same small wooden house she built at Mankiller Flats in 1976. Later in the morning, she would drive her old brown station wagon to Tahlequah, the headquarters of the Cherokee Nation, and set to work in her government office, a light blue room decorated with art from a variety of traditions—both Indian and non-Indian—and informal photographs of her daughters and grandchildren.

Like any public official, Mankiller found that her days were usually packed with meetings, public appearances, phone calls, and decisions. Her job, she once said, was like "running a little country and a big corporation at the same time." She was responsible both to the Cherokee tribe—some 140,000 people—and to the Cherokee Nation, where more than 1,200 employees managed the tribe's finances and ran a wide range of programs.

Because she was the first woman to serve as principal chief of the Cherokee Nation, Wilma Mankiller was also a minor celebrity. She was named *Ms.* magazine's Woman of the Year in 1987, and in the years that followed she continued to give interviews and to speak at institutions around the nation. She got used to answering questions

Standing in front of the Oklahoma state seal, Principal Chief Wilma Mankiller looks toward a future of leadership and service.

In her office at the Cherokee Nation, Mankiller holds a poster commemorating a state conference on the status of women.

about her family name. Because she was called "Mankiller," she noticed, people would often expect her to be aggressive, even hostile, and they were surprised to find her a fairly calm, quiet person. She would usually explain that the name had its origins in a Cherokee warrior tradition, but, she once said, "sometimes I tell people it's a nickname . . . and I earned it."

Though her duties as principle chief kept her very busy, Mankiller decided to maintain an open-door policy both at her home and at her Tahlequah office, encouraging members of the tribe to call on her with their problems and opinions. She did her best to give each of them her full attention. For at least one Cherokee woman, Janice Ballou, Mankiller's commitment to personal assistance made a big difference. In the late 1980s, when

Ballou applied to the Cherokee Nation for college financial aid, it was Wilma Mankiller who saw that she got it. Ballou recalled:

> I was just going to go part time. I have four kids, and my twins were only about two then. I was applying late, so I called up the complex and talked to Wilma. I just asked her if there was any money available, even just for mileage, or gas, just to get me started. A couple of weeks later I got a letter and a full-time grant. I just about fell over.

Janice Ballou went on to study education, with a minor in music. When she graduated, she became the director of a choir at a Cherokee school. "We sing in Cherokee and wear traditional Cherokee dress," Ballou told an interviewer. "We've performed in a lot of different places. Last year we performed in Washington, D.C. The Cherokee Nation—Wilma and Charlie themselves, and the council—sent donations to help with the trip."

Mankiller also stayed in touch with the people in her tribe by organizing meetings in remote areas, just as she had when she was the director of community development. "She'll come down and just have dinner," Debbie Smoke, the former mayor of Spavinaw in Mayes County, Oklahoma, has said of her. "We get everyone together at the senior citizen center for an informal potluck dinner. People gripe and complain and Wilma listens. If there's something she can do, she will."

James Morrison, another strong supporter, told one interviewer:

> She's what I call a "grassroots chief." You'll see her anywhere in the 14 counties of the Cherokee Nation. She's just out there with the people. She'll go to the hog fries. Little kids are always hanging around her. She just sits there amongst everybody, and listens to their concerns.

To her gratification, Mankiller often found that the communities she had worked with earlier in her career at the Cherokee Nation were continuing her initiatives on their own. "In the town I live in we wanted to build a community center," Debbie Smoke recounted. "We wrote a proposal and got funded by the state. Then Wilma helped us get matching funds from a private foundation. We have a real nice community building now."

Mankiller continued to impress her colleagues and other Cherokee citizens with her detailed knowledge of tribal affairs and her ability to make decisions in the midst of many competing needs. At a meeting with the board of directors of the Cherokee Heritage Center, Mankiller made it clear that while the center was important to the tribe as a symbol of Cherokee culture and tradition, the Cherokee Nation could not fund it completely. She announced that the tribe would give the center a generous grant, but that the money was not to be used for operating costs. Her strategy obliged the

William and Debbie Smoke, two of the principal chief's loyal supporters, join their daughter Audra after she is crowned Miss Cherokee in 1988.

Heritage Center to bring in its own share of income by attracting more visitors.

While Mankiller continued to emphasize the importance of increasing the earnings of the Cherokee Nation, she also remained selective about the enterprises she was willing to endorse. In the late 1980s, the federal government exempted Indian tribes from certain gambling laws, allowing them to operate gambling facilities on tribal land. Many tribes took advantage of this new opportunity to raise money for health care, housing, and other needs. Although Mankiller supported the right of these tribes to make their own decisions, she remained cautious about involving the Cherokee Nation, citing studies that showed a connection between gambling and crime.

In the same spirit, Mankiller asked the tribal council to pass a resolution requiring all businesses brought into the Cherokee Nation to be screened for environmental safety. "The businesses we want to attract have got to have good environmental records," she told the council. "It's not worth the long-term damage to the environment for the short-term benefit of providing jobs." In the late 1980s, the federal government began asking Indian tribes to consider storing nuclear waste. When the request came to the Cherokee Nation, Mankiller flatly rejected it.

Mankiller tried to stimulate the local economy by attracting safe, profitable industries that would offer the Cherokees jobs. Jay Hanna, president of Banc First in Tahlequah, worked closely with her in the effort. "Probably one of the greatest challenges we face in this area is having ample employment," he said in an interview. "It's the very thing that took Wilma's family to California, and more than 30 years later we're still struggling to create good quality jobs for our people."

Mankiller created the Private Industry Council, a body that brought representatives from private businesses, government agencies, and the Cherokee Nation together to discuss ways to encourage industries to locate in northeastern Oklahoma. "The chief takes a holistic approach to the economy here," explained Hanna, the council's cochairman. "She recognizes that we are a unique culture, a unique people, but at the same time we are citizens of the state of Oklahoma and of the United States and that whatever is good for northeastern Oklahoma is good for the Cherokee Nation."

Under Mankiller's leadership, the tribe also continued to build new businesses of its own, including an electronic harness and cabling company, a hydroelectric plant, and a nursery. Mankiller also established a job corps center that provided employment training, as well as programs offering technical assistance and financial backing to Cherokees trying to start their own small businesses.

As she worked to build up the communities around her, Mankiller generally enjoyed the support of her people. But a small faction of Cherokees, called the United Keetoowah Band, opposed both her leadership and the Cherokee Nation as a whole. Formed in the 1930s, the band took its name from a traditional Cherokee religious society called the Keetoowahs. The group included some 7,000 members and had its own constitution. For more than 50 years, Cherokees who belonged to the United Keetoowah Band could also be members of the much larger Cherokee Nation. In the 1980s, however, the leaders of the United Keetoowah Band began to require its members to withdraw from the Cherokee Nation. Declaring themselves the true Cherokee tribe, the members of the United Keetoowah Band set up their own businesses and even their own police force.

Like her predecessor, Ross Swimmer, Mankiller dealt with the United Keetoowah Band by fighting its claims in court. The band's members clearly rejected her lead-

Accompanied by supporters, Mankiller prepares to dig a symbolic shovelful of earth at the opening of the Talking Leaves Job Corps Center, an organization she established to provide Cherokees with vocational training.

ership, but she took their protests in stride. As Mankiller herself put it, "It's hard to rattle me."

Toward the end of her four-year term, Mankiller also had health problems to contend with. In June 1990, the condition she had inherited from her father worsened, and she was forced to undergo a kidney transplant, a dangerous operation for both the patient and the donor. Mankiller's brother Donald had agreed to serve as donor that spring. Later, Mankiller wrote:

> I know how hard that decision was for him to make. There are obviously no words to thank him for his sacrifice. As he had been all my life when he worked so hard along with my father to put food on the table and shoes on our feet, my big brother Don was once again a hero.

The operation went well, and with her usual energy and determination, Mankiller went back to her demanding schedule only a short while later.

Mankiller's many commitments as principal chief meant that she had to travel frequently. It was her responsibility to represent her tribe in Oklahoma City—

the capital of Oklahoma—and in Washington, D.C., where she met regularly with the BIA and congressional leaders. As principal chief, it was her job to lobby the state and federal governments for funding and for the passage of laws that would benefit her tribe. Although Mankiller did not particularly enjoy this aspect of her work, she found that she had a talent for it. Government officials admired her commitment, her knowledge of the law, and her compelling personality. They also knew that she was capable of bringing about real change for her people.

Between 1987 and 1991, the Cherokees made great strides in health care and education. The tribe built new health clinics in several counties, set up a mobile eye-care clinic, and created an ambulance service. Mankiller's government established a Head Start program to provide early education for Cherokee children and another program for adult education.

These achievements set the Cherokees apart from many other tribes and helped them compete successfully for more funding. Mankiller's willingness to cooperate with state and federal governments also distinguished the Cherokee Nation from other tribes. George Bearpaw, executive director of tribal operations at the Cherokee Nation, described Mankiller's approach in a 1992 interview: "We're not isolated. We work with other governments on a daily basis and we cooperate to the extent that we can. Most other tribes don't do that. The chief doesn't back down from a fight, but she doesn't want us to create adversarial relationships unnecessarily."

Mankiller's cooperative approach has served the Cherokees well. In 1990—while she lay in a Boston hospital recuperating from her kidney transplant—she signed a new self-governance agreement with the United States, an arrangement that increased the Cherokee Nation's control over its share of federal funding.

Mankiller regarded the agreement as a significant step toward one of her basic goals: that the Cherokee Nation would assume complete responsibility for its resources, as it had in the 19th century.

Despite her dedication, when it came time for Mankiller to decide whether to run for another term as principal chief in 1991, she found herself weighing the matter carefully. "I love my work, but committing to another four years was a big decision," she later said. Ultimately, however, she decided to run again; as principal chief of the Cherokees, she realized, there was still much she could achieve.

The Cherokee people agreed. On June 15, 1991, Mankiller was reelected—this time on a first ballot, with 83 percent of the vote. As she entered her second term in office, she continued in her role as a spokesperson and role model, not only for her own tribe, but for Indians across the country. One of Wilma Mankiller's abiding principles is a firm belief in the power of Native Americans—a power that can lead them anywhere if only they realize it is there. "My life may be unusual, but not to the Indian world," she pointed out after her reelection. "My ability to survive personal crises is really a mark of the character of my people." Mankiller continued:

> A big part of setting the stage for having people take control of their own lives and solve their own problems is getting people to believe they can. Our folks are a long way away from uniformly believing that, after a couple hundred years of being told that other people have the best ideas for us.

In a life filled with achievements, Principal Chief Wilma Mankiller has named the one she would like to be remembered for most: that she helped the Cherokee Nation, and perhaps all Native Americans, to regain their faith in themselves.

CHRONOLOGY

1945 Born in Stilwell, Oklahoma, on November 18

1957 Moves with family to San Francisco under federal relocation program

1963 Marries Hugo Olaya

1964 Gives birth to daughter Felicia

1966 Gives birth to second daughter, Gina

1969 Indian activists occupy Alcatraz Island; Mankiller joins Indian rights movement

1975 Divorces Hugo Olaya

1976 Returns with daughters to Oklahoma

1977 Becomes economic-stimulus coordinator at Cherokee Nation

1979 Sustains serious injuries in car accident

1980 Undergoes surgery for myasthenia gravis

1981 Begins Bell community project

1982 Founds Community Development Department of the Cherokee Nation

1983 Elected deputy chief of the Cherokee Nation

1985 Mankiller becomes first female principal chief of the Cherokee Nation

1986 Marries Charlie Soap

1987 Elected to four-year term as principal chief; named *Ms.* magazine's Woman of the Year

1990 Undergoes kidney transplant; signs self-governance agreement with United States

1991 Reelected principal chief

1993 Publishes autobiography, *Mankiller: A Chief and Her People*

FURTHER READING

Awtakta, Marilou. "Rebirth of a Nation." *Southern Style,* October 1988.

Devlin, Jeanne M. "Hail to the Chief." *Oklahoma Today,* January/February 1990.

Ehle, John. *Trail of Tears: The Rise and Fall of the Cherokee Nation.* New York: Doubleday, 1988.

Fixico, Donald L. *Urban Indians.* New York: Chelsea House, 1991.

Fortunate Eagle, Adam. *Alcatraz! Alcatraz!* Berkeley: Heyday Books, 1992.

Glassman, Bruce. *Wilma Mankiller: Chief of the Cherokee Nation.* Woodbridge, CT: Blackbirch Press, 1992.

Josephy, Alvin M., Jr. *Red Power: The American Indian's Fight for Freedom.* Lincoln: University of Nebraska Press, 1971.

Mankiller, Wilma, and Michael Wallis. *Mankiller: A Chief and Her People.* New York: St. Martin's Press, 1993.

Perdue, Theda. *The Cherokee.* New York: Chelsea House, 1989.

Steiner, Stan. *The New Indians.* New York: Delta Books, 1968.

Wallace, Michelle. "Wilma Mankiller." *Ms.,* January 1988.

INDEX

Alcatraz! Alcatraz! (Fortunate Eagle), 18
Alcatraz Island, 11–13, 15, 16–20, 21
Allotment policy, 33, 34, 62
American Indian Movement (AIM), 15, 16
   San Francisco branch, 15

Ballou, Janice, 98, 99
Bearpaw, George, 104
Bell, Oklahoma, 69–71, 86
Blackfoot Indians, 56
Bratskellers restaurant, 18
Bureau of Indian Affairs (BIA), 20, 39, 40, 83, 104
   allotment policy, 33, 34, 62
   self-determination policy, 21, 55
   termination policy, 14, 15, 20, 21, 39–42, 57

California, 17, 41, 42, 52, 53, 64, 101
Chemotherapy, 68
Cherokee Heritage Center, 81, 100, 101
Cherokee Indians, 23, 42, 58, 61, 63, 64, 68, 75, 76, 77, 86, 89, 98
   Bird clan, 26
   Blue clan, 26
   Deer clan, 26
   full-blood–mixed-blood controversy, 79–83
   history, 13, 14, 25–35, 36, 80
   Keetoowahs, 102
   language, 25, 28, 35, 80, 81, 91, 94
   Long Hair clan, 26
   medicine, 65, 67
   Paint clan, 26
   political structure, 26, 29, 30, 32, 62, 82, 83, 85, 86
   and Trail of Tears, 13, 31, 35
   United Keetoowah Band, 102
   Wild Potato clan, 26
   Wolf clan, 26. *See also* Cherokee Nation
Cherokee Nation, 30, 33, 34, 35, 62, 68, 73, 74, 77, 82, 83, 85, 86, 89, 91, 93, 95, 97, 99, 100, 101, 102, 104, 105
   Community Development Department of, 71
   Tribal Council of, 77, 78, 85, 88, 101. *See also* Cherokee Indians
Cherokee Nation complex, 63
Chickasaw Indians, 28, 39. *See also* Five Civilized Tribes
Choctaw Indians, 26, 28, 31. *See also* Five Civilized Tribes
Cooper, Betty, 56, 57
Creek Indians, 26, 27, 28, 31. *See also* Five Civilized Tribes

Daly City, California, 43, 44, 45

East Oakland, California, 55

Five Civilized Tribes, 28, 30

Fortunate Eagle, Adam, 18

Georgia, 30
Government, U.S., 11, 12, 13, 15, 27, 31, 33, 54, 69, 76, 89, 101, 104

Hanna, Jay, 101, 102
Head Start program, 104

Indian Child Welfare Act, 57
Indian Housing Authority, 86
Indian Removal Act, 30
Indian Territory, 13, 14, 31, 32, 33, 34, 35, 80. *See also* Oklahoma
Institute for Cherokee Literacy, 81

Jackson, Andrew, 30
Johnson, Lyndon B., 62

Keetowahs, 102
Kingfisher, 27

Mankiller, Charles (father), 13, 14, 15, 23, 24, 25, 26, 35, 39, 40, 41, 42, 44, 47, 51, 52, 53, 80, 81, 103
Mankiller, Donald (brother), 42, 43
Mankiller, Frances (sister), 47
Mankiller, Irene (mother), 23, 24, 35, 40, 41, 42, 44, 47, 51, 52, 59, 61
Mankiller, John (grandfather), 34, 61
Mankiller, Robert (brother), 45
Mankiller, Wilma Pearl
   and Alcatraz occupation, 11,

109

12, 16, 17, 51, 53
autobiography, 36, 44, 47
birth, 23
car accident, 65–67, 91
childhood, 14, 23–25, 35–46, 91
community activism in California, 11, 12, 16, 17, 21, 51, 57
community activism in Oklahoma, 63–64, 68, 69–71, 74, 86, 91
as deputy chief of the Cherokee Nation, 73–83, 94
develops Indian Child Welfare Act, 56–57
divorce, 55
education, 15, 36, 37, 42, 43, 44, 45, 46, 48, 53, 65, 80
and full-blood–mixed-blood controversy, 79–83
illnesses, 52, 67, 68, 91, 93, 103, 104
kidney transplant, 103–4
marriages, 47, 86, 88
moves to San Francisco, 39–42
Ms. magazine's Woman of the Year, 1987, 97
president of Tribal Council, 77–78
principal chief of Cherokee Nation, 83–105
return to Oklahoma, 58–61
and sexism, 74, 75, 76, 77, 79, 94
Mankiller: A Chief and Her People, 36
Mankiller Flats, Oklahoma, 24, 25, 34, 35, 40, 59, 61, 69, 88, 91, 93

Monterey, California, 51
Morris, Sherry, 65
Morrison, James, 92, 99
Ms. magazine, 97
Muscular dystrophy, 67, 68
Myasthenia gravis, 68

National Indian Youth Council, 20
Native American Youth Center, 55
Nixon, Richard, 21, 55, 62

Oakland, California, 40, 55, 56, 57, 61
Oaks Indian Center, 92
Ohlone Indians, 12
Oklahoma, 14, 25, 30, 34, 35, 39, 40, 41, 42, 44, 52, 61, 62, 69, 80, 86, 89, 92, 99, 102, 104. *See also* Indian Territory
Olaya de Bardi, Felicia (daughter), 11, 47, 53, 56, 57, 58, 61, 93
Olaya de Bardi, Gina (daughter), 11, 47, 53, 56, 57, 58, 61, 93
Olaya de Bardi, Hector Hugo (husband), 11, 47, 48, 53, 55

Pit River Indians, 17, 53, 54
Polycystic kidney disease, 52
Private Industry Council, 101

Reagan, Ronald, 83, 91
Relocation policy. *See* Termination policy
Riverbank, California, 40, 44, 45
Rocky Mountain, Oklahoma, 23

Rocky Mountain Elementary School, 36, 42
Ross, John, 30, 31

San Francisco, California, 11, 14, 15, 17, 40, 41, 42, 43, 45, 51, 53, 54, 80, 91
San Francisco Indian Center, 15, 16, 43, 45
San Francisco State University, 47, 48, 53, 56
Self-determination policy, 21, 55
Seminole Indians, 28, 31. *See also* Five Civilized Tribes
Sequoyah, 28
Skyline Junior College, 48
Smoke, Debbie, 99, 100
Soap, Charlie (second husband), 86, 88, 94, 99
Stickball, 36, 81
Stilwell, Oklahoma, 39, 49, 52, 61
Stomp Ground, 35
Swimmer, Ross, 62, 73, 74, 83, 85, 88, 89, 102

Tahlequah, Oklahoma, 63, 97, 98, 102
Termination policy, 14, 15, 20, 21, 39–42, 57
Trail of Tears, 13, 31, 35

United Bay Area Council of American Indian Affairs, Inc., 20
United Keetowah Band, 102
University of Arkansas, 65
Urban Indian Resource Center, 56

Ward, Nancy, 27
Wheeler, Perry, 88, 89, 94

110

PICTURE CREDITS

Courtesy of American Indian Child Resource Center, Oakland, CA: p. 50; Archives & Manuscripts Division, Oklahoma Historical Society: pp. 29, 32, 63, 90; ©Jim Argo: p. 96; The Bettmann Archive: pp. 43, 60; Cherokee Nation Photo: pp. 2, 22, 26, 38, 70, 72, 75, 84, 87, 106; Tom Gilbert/World Publishing: p. 98; ©Ilka Hartman/photo courtesy of Intertribal Friendship House, Oakland, CA: p. 58; Library of Congress: pp. 28 (neg. #LC-USZ62-1292), 33 (neg. #LC-USZ62-11487); ©Betty Jane Nevis/photo courtesy of Intertribal Friendship House, Oakland, CA: p. 54; Courtesy of the Oakland Convention and Visitors Bureau: p. 56; Courtesy of William and Deborah Smoke: pp. 93, 100; Special Collections Division, University of Arkansas Libraries, Fayetteville: p. 66; April Stone/*Tahlequah Daily Press:* p. 103; UPI/Bettmann: pp. 10, 12, 19, 46, 64, 82; John Vaughan Library, University Archives, Northeastern State University, Tahlequah, OK: p. 78; Western History Collections, University of Oklahoma Libraries: p. 34.

ACKNOWLEDGMENTS

The author wishes to thank the following people for submitting to interviews for this book: Janice Ballou, director of the Cherokee Choir at Kenwood School, Kenwood, OK; George Bearpaw, Cherokee Nation executive director of tribal operations; Betty Cooper, director of the American Indian Family Healing Center, Oakland, CA; Jay Hanna, president of Banc First, Tahlequah, OK; James Morrison, director of the Oaks Children Center, Oaks, OK; Debbie Smoke, former mayor of Spavinaw, Mayes County, OK; and William Smoke, member of the Cherokee Nation Tribal Council. Also gratefully acknowledged is the assistance of Lynn Howard, Cherokee Nation communications director; Kim Maloy, Cherokee Nation public affairs special project manager; Susan Lobo, director of the Community History Project at the Intertribal Friendship House, Oakland, CA; and Clara Sue Kidwell, associate professor of Native American Studies at University of California Berkeley.

MELISSA SCHWARZ is a book editor with a longtime interest in the American West. She is the author of *Cochise* and *Geronimo* in the Chelsea House NORTH AMERICAN INDIANS OF ACHIEVEMENT series. Ms. Schwarz currently lives in Berkeley, California.

W. DAVID BAIRD is the Howard A. White Professor of History at Pepperdine University in Malibu, California. He holds a Ph.D. from the University of Oklahoma and was formerly on the faculty of history at the University of Arkansas, Fayetteville, and Oklahoma State University. He has served as president of both the Western History Association, a professional organization, and Phi Alpha Theta, the international honor society for students of history. Dr. Baird is also the author of *The Quapaw Indians: A History of the Downstream People* and *Peter Pitchlynn: Chief of the Choctaws* and the editor of *A Creek Warrior of the Confederacy: The Autobiography of Chief G. W. Grayson*.